THE OCCASIONS OF POETRY

Books by Thom Gunn

Fighting Terms
The Sense of Movement
My Sad Captains
Positives
Touch
Poems 1950–1966
Moly
Jack Straw's Castle
Selected Poems 1950–1975
The Passages of Joy

THE OCCASIONS OF POETRY

Essays in Criticism and Autobiography

by
THOM GUNN

Edited and with an Introduction by
CLIVE WILMER

faber and faber

This collection first published in 1982
by Faber and Faber Limited
3 Queen Square, London WC1N 3AU
Printed in Great Britain by
Willmer Brothers Limited
Rock Ferry, Merseyside

British Library Cataloguing in Publication Data

Gunn, Thom
The occasions of poetry
1. English poetry—History and criticism—Addresses,
essays, lectures
2. Gunn, Thom   3. Poets, English—20th century—Biography
I. Title   II. Wilmer, Clive
821'.009   PR503

ISBN 0-571-11733-3

Contents

Acknowledgements

The essays in this collection originally appeared in the following publications, to whose editors and publishers thanks are due.

'A New World' [first published as 'William Carlos Williams']: *Encounter* XXV, 1 (July 1965).

'The Early Snyder' [first published as two separate pieces]: 'Interpenetrating Things', *Agenda* IV, 3–4 (Summer 1966); and 'Waking with Wonder', *Listener*, 2 May 1968.

'Fulke Greville', Introduction to *Selected Poems of Fulke Greville*, ed. Thom Gunn, London (Faber and Faber), 1968.

'Hardy and the Ballads', *Agenda* X, 2–3 (Spring–Summer 1972).

'Ben Jonson', Introduction to *Ben Jonson*, selected by Thom Gunn, Harmondsworth (Penguin), 1974.

'Homosexuality in Robert Duncan's Poetry', *Robert Duncan, Scales of the Marvellous*, ed. Robert J. Bertholf and Ian W. Reid, New York (New Directions), 1979.

'New Lineaments', *Poetry* CXXI, 4 (January 1973).

'Immersions', *Thames Poetry* I, 2 (Summer 1976).

'A Heroic Enterprise', *San Francisco Review of Books* V, 3 (August 1979).

'Writing a Poem' [originally untitled], *Corgi Modern Poets in Focus: 5*, ed. Dannie Abse, London (Corgi Books), 1973.

'My Suburban Muse', *Worlds: Seven Modern Poets*, ed. Geoffrey Summerfield, Harmondsworth (Penguin), 1974.

'Cambridge in the Fifties' (originally untitled), *My Cambridge*, ed. Ronald Hayman, London (Robson Books), 1977.

ACKNOWLEDGEMENTS

'My Life up to Now', Biographical Introduction to *Thom Gunn: A Bibliography, 1940–1978*, compiled by Jack W. C. Hagstrom and George Bixby, London (Bertram Rota), 1979.

Minor revisions have sometimes been made in the interests of style and/or long-term relevance.

I should like to express my special thanks to Jack W. C. Hagstrom for letting me see the 'Periodicals' section of the Thom Gunn *Bibliography* prior to publication.

C.W.

This book has been published with financial assistance from the Arts Council of Great Britain.

Introduction

Writing in one of these essays about his friendship with Robert Duncan and the mutual influence that has come of it, Thom Gunn remarks that 'it may sound rather as if Fulke Greville and Shelley had been contemporaries capable of learning from each other. Would that they had been.' This welcoming of what he recognizes as an improbable influence is characteristic. Gunn is quite consciously a writer of contrasts, who has drawn on a wide range of influences and modes. But his work none the less impresses the careful reader with its underlying consistency. He made his name, after all, as a master of rigorously traditional verse forms, and he continues to excel in them, but he has since become hardly less accomplished in a variety of 'open' forms and the verse is no less shapely. His approach is at root impersonal: his first person, like Ralegh's or Jonson's or Hardy's, is unquestionably that of a particular man, but a man who expects his individuality to be of interest in so far as it is a quality the reader shares with him. (It is true that an individual life-style provides the poetry with much of its subject matter, but even in his youth the 'confident poseur' maintained a modest relation to the language and to the conventions of his art.) His work, which has done much to dispel the critical orthodoxy that abstract language is inimical to poetry, has become over the years increasingly sensuous in detail, reflecting preoccupations that were there from the beginning, though not at first as qualities of the language. For this most chaste of modern poets is a philosophical hedonist—rather like Camus, of all modern moralists the one he appears to value most.

The most interesting contrast of all, perhaps, is connected with his sense of the past. What strikes us most immediately in Gunn's poems—what made him famous in fact—is their contained energy. Yet he is also, without falling into academicism, a highly literary poet, and his literariness, far from being a limitation, may well be the main source of his strength. Gunn's vulnerability, as Donald Davie has said in praise of him, has much to do with his renunciation of the 'glibly deprecating ironies' that insulated so many of the fifties' poets from the full range of poetic possibility. In order to escape such 'facile knowingness' and the phase of British culture that it expressed, Gunn went back to the youth of English poetry 'to discover that phase of British English—Donne's, Marlowe's, above all Shakespeare's—in which the language could register without embarrassment the frankly heroic'. And in his mature work, says Davie, 'The Renaissance styles—of life more than of writing—are invoked . . . not to judge the tawdry present, nor to keep it at arm's length, but on the contrary so as to comprehend it in a way that extends to it not just compassion but dignity. . . .'[1] The only tradition in the English language that shares this verbal innocence is that of American poetry since Whitman, with all its vulnerability and spaciousness. Gunn, who has lived in the United States since 1955, has nourished himself on that tradition too—so it is perhaps no accident that most of the essays in this collection deal with American or Renaissance writers.

An example of what Davie has in mind is to be found in an attractive and funny love poem called 'An Amorous Debate'. The medium is free verse and the approach owes something to the Ed Dorn of *Gunslinger*; the protagonists, Leather Kid and Fleshly, clearly belong to modern California; but the poem's convention is that of such older philosophical and amorous encounters as Donne's 'The Extasie' and Lord Herbert's 'Ode upon a Question Moved'. These literary echoes do not encumber the poem or detract from its vitality and wit. We do not need to notice, for example, that the last lines appear to have been borrowed from the French Renaissance poet Maurice Scève, though it adds to our delight in the poem if we do.

Behind 'An Amorous Debate' is to be found a continuing preoccupation with neo-Platonic notions of love and the Petrarchan conventions through which they have been expressed in poetry. Gunn is interested in these notions, as his essay on Fulke Greville shows, not so much for their own sake as because they are an

[1] Review of Gunn's *Selected Poems 1950–1975*, *New Republic*, 13 Oct. 1979, pp. 37–8.

important instance of the tension that must exist between the truth of experience and the artifice of art. He admires the way Greville uses the conventions so as to contradict them in the interests of truth. In the same essay, the reader will find what I take to be the source of an image in the poem 'Jack Straw's Castle': Little-ease, 'the cell where one cannot stand, sit, or lie', as a metaphor for moral catatonia, was first used by Greville in *Caelica*, CII. Gunn compares his use of it to an almost identical image in Camus's *La Chute*. The passage provides us with a useful literary gloss on Gunn's poem and similar glosses will be found elsewhere in this collection. I cite these links between Gunn's poetry and the most nearly scholarly of his essays to show how his sense of the past feeds his imagination. When he was an undergraduate, he tells us, 'Donne and Shakespeare spoke living language' to him; 'they were writers I could see as bearing upon the present, upon my own activities'. His criticism is interesting for what, indirectly, it tells us about his poetry, but it is still more valuable for the way his own experience of writing illuminates what he reads. He is, quite simply, a marvellous 'reader' of other men's verse.

The aspect of literary practice which engages Gunn's critical intelligence most frequently and most fruitfully is the relation of a poet's words to the subject matter that calls them forth. He speaks of this near the beginning of his essay on Ben Jonson. (He is defending Jonson against the charge that his poetry is merely 'occasional'.)

> ... in fact all poetry is occasional: whether the occasion is an external event like a birthday or a declaration of war, whether it is an occasion of the imagination, or whether it is in some sort of combination of the two. (After all, the external may lead to the internal occasions.) The occasion in all cases—literal or imaginary—is the starting point, only, of a poem, but it should be a starting point to which the poet must in some sense stay true. The truer he is to it, the closer he sticks to what for him is its authenticity, the more he will be able to draw from it in the adventures that it produces, adventures that consist of the experience of writing.

The first loyalty of writers like Jonson who are 'true to their occasions' must be not to the self, nor to some prior ideology or faith, nor even to the imagination, but to the facts of experience. This accounts for the near-heroic status accorded by Gunn to William Carlos Williams. The virtues of Williams's poetry 'derive from a habitual sympathy, by which he recognizes his own energy' in a variety of other lives; 'it is a humane action to attempt the rendering of a thing, person, or experience in the exact terms of its existence.' This is to say, in effect, that Williams's greatness lies in the fact that, as a poet, he is more interested in the world than in himself, though a self is always present behind the poems as the source of value in them. Hardy, similarly, is free from falsifying rhetoric and posturing, being concerned to present things as they are, even if this sometimes necessitates inelegance of movement or diction. Gunn praises him, too, for allowing himself to come across in his poetry as a 'general' figure. By contrast, when faced with those poets, vatic or confessional, who treat the self as a marketable product, Gunn is moved to contempt.

The occasions of poetry, however, are only starting points. They constitute the 'shape' of experience, but the task of a poet is to seek out its 'content'. Gunn employs a variety of related metaphors to describe the journey between the two: exploration and adventure, and the related images of looting and conquest. These metaphors unite poets as diverse as Robert Duncan and Yvor Winters. Duncan, indeed, as becomes so Blakeian a writer, is more interested in the process than the result:

> What Duncan has stressed is the importance of the *act* of writing. It is a reach into the unknown, an adventuring into places you cannot have predicted, where you may find yourself using limbs and organs you didn't know you possessed.

Winters, by contrast, as poet and as critic, was more concerned with the finished product, with what he was to call—it is the title of his last book—*Forms of Discovery*, though even there the emphasis is on the way the form contains or articulates the process of discovery.

Winters's place in this outline needs special emphasis, if only because Gunn has written nothing about him that seemed worth reprinting. It is a pity he hasn't because no other writer has affected him so profoundly. His influence on these essays can be seen in their style and their values and even sometimes in their choice of subject. It was Winters who first introduced Gunn to the poetry of Williams.

And who else so consistently championed Jonson and Greville and Hardy as major poets in the tradition of what Gunn calls 'the reflective lyric'? In one of Gunn's uncollected articles, he tells how Winters rejected the experimental free verse of his youth (poems which embody 'a view of life as a series of ecstatically perceived fragments') in favour of the rational formality for which he is better known. Gunn quotes the early poem 'Quod Tegit Omnia' :

> Adventurer in
> living fact, the poet
> mounts into the spring,
> upon his tongue the taste of
> air becoming body : is
> embedded in this crystalline
> precipitate of time.

Since that time [Gunn continues] he came to view the writing of poetry as 'a technique of comprehension', involving full use of the rational powers and moral judgement that he had deliberately avoided in his earliest work. The poet may still be 'embedded' in his subject matter, but he now tries to view it in a context which can enable him to understand it. The discipline of his style does not reject experience—rather it is a means of simultaneously conveying it, in all its richness and variety, and evaluating it, since the conveying has little meaning without the evaluation.[1]

He might have added that Winters never quite loses that sense of the poet as an 'Adventurer in/living fact'. Winters's conception of what a poem is, however, now seems to Gunn excessively rigid. Towards the end of his life, Winters condemned Williams as 'a foolish and ignorant man'.[2] This may account in part for Gunn's feeling that Winters's theory is to some extent vitiated by 'an increasing distaste for the particulars of existence'. But Gunn has retained his attachment to Winters's view of poetry as 'a technique of comprehension'—so much so that he has adapted it to a kind of

---

[1] *The Concise Encyclopaedia of English and American Poets and Poetry*, eds. Stephen Spender and Donald Hall (2nd edition, revised), London, 1970, pp. 324–5.
[2] Yvor Winters, *Forms of Discovery*, Denver, 1967, p. 319.

poetry, much of it preoccupied with particularity, that Winters ultimately felt bound to reject.[1]

If the process of poetry, then, is adventure or exploration, its goal must be 'understanding'. This is a word which recurs so often in Winters and Gunn that we are justified in suspecting its meaning to be less obvious than we might at first have thought. Gunn comments on Ben Jonson's use of the word in his epigram 'To the Reader':

> Pray thee, take care, that tak'st my booke in hand,
> To reade it well : that is, to understand.

'The process of understanding', says Gunn, amounts to something 'more than the business of comprehending the text . . . Understanding means taking [the poems] to heart, means—ultimately—*acting* on them.' Of course, he is referring not to the business of understanding life but to the effect of literature. But to apply the word 'understand' to experience at all is, in a sense, to draw an analogy between life and books. If we study life, we can learn from it; our chances of acting on experience are improved. As Winters said of history, though he might equally have said it of personal experience, 'Unless we understand the history that produced us, we are determined by that history; we may be determined at any event, but the understanding gives us a chance.'[2]

In recent years, Gunn's interest in American poetry has moved away from the traditionalism Winters stood for towards the more loosely informal writing that acknowledges Pound and Williams as its masters. This book, which begins with an essay written in 1965, may be read in part as a record of that shift in emphasis. During this period Gunn seems to have broadened his use of the word 'understanding'. For Jonson and Winters it was the *sine qua non* of poetry and implied a reduction of experience to generalized formulae. Gunn now argues that poetry is 'an attempt to *grasp*, with grasp meaning both to *take hold of* in a first bid at possession, and also to *understand*'. A grasp of particulars is now quite as important to him as the formulation of propositions, and it entails a concreteness of language that twenty years ago had seemed beside the point. This has nothing to do with metaphor or symbol or correlatives for private

[1] For a fuller account of this, see my 'Definition and Flow : A Personal Reading of Thom Gunn', *PN Review* V, 3, pp. 51–7.
[2] Yvor Winters, op. cit., p. xix.

emotion. What he values is the precise rendering of physical fact *as it is*, in all its 'thinginess'. Yet when he says of Gary Snyder, the master of this kind of writing, that 'like most serious poets he is mainly concerned at finding himself on a barely known planet in an almost unknown universe, where he must attempt to create and discover meanings', we realize that Gunn has not moved far from the Wintersian position, for he sees Snyder's poetry as a matter of exploration, discovery and understanding. A poem like 'Mid-August at Sourdough Mountain Lookout' is not merely the record of a feeling or sensation. In attempting to notate the particulars of experience accurately, Snyder guides us gently into territory we all share. Language, after all, is a common property. When we are persuaded, through language, of the truth of a perception, we have entered the realm of generality : we have stumbled on meaning. Gunn's special talent as a critic lies in his ability to show how, as we read, we move in this way from occasion to meaning.

The essays I have selected for this book were written over the last fifteen years. Gunn had previously done a good deal of book review-ing, notably for the *London Magazine* in the days of John Lehmann (the first editor to publish his work extensively) and between 1958 and 1964 for the *Yale Review*. Many of these reviews are stimulating and incisive in detail but ultimately too ephemeral for a collection of this kind. The influence first of F. R. Leavis and then of Winters is often excessive and, as Gunn admits in a recent memoir, his judgements are sometimes too hasty, too dependent on first impres-sions. Occasionally, when he is recommending American writers un-known to the British public at that time—his reviews of Winters and Wallace Stevens, for example[1]—the articles have a certain historical interest, but they are little more, finally, than introductions and brief summaries. It was when Gunn gave up the regular practice of book reviewing that he began to write criticism of lasting interest, and it is at this point that the present collection begins.

Cambridge, 1980   CLIVE WILMER

[1] *London Magazine*, VII, 10, pp. 64–6, and III, 4, pp. 81–4, respectively.

I

CRITICISM

A NEW WORLD: The Poetry
of William Carlos Williams

At one time it must have seemed as if T. S. Eliot and William Carlos Williams had divided between them the gifts of their friend Ezra Pound—Eliot taking the polish of *Mauberley*, the emphasis on a constantly shifting and mysterious tone, the sense of dislocated internal drama, and Williams taking the wistful sentiment of *Cathay*, the emphasis on the image, and the concern for clear delineation of the external world. Though this would be an over-simplification, it is true that they did originally share a common meeting-place in Pound, the potentiality of each being strengthened by this man who, both in his poetry and in that of his friends, was the originator of what we uncomfortably call Modernism.

Yet because the gifts they took were so different they developed in decisively different directions. Williams, in fact, soon came to see Eliot as the Enemy. In his *Autobiography* he speaks of *The Waste Land* as 'the great catastrophe to our letters', and elsewhere he says of *Prufrock*: 'I had a violent feeling that Eliot had betrayed what I believed in. He was looking backward; I was looking forward. . . . I felt he had rejected America.'

Williams had his mystique of what is American and what isn't, but as a gloss we may take his prose book of 1925, *In the American Grain*. America is here seen as a New World in spirit as well as in fact: most of the colonists made the great mistake of attempting to understand it and even remould it only in terms of the Old, America being 'a living flame' compared to the 'dead ash' of England. But there were some who had the ability to see what was there:

Daniel Boone, for instance, who found in the wilderness a 'power to strengthen every form of energy that would be voluptuous, passionate, possessive in that place which he opened'; or the Père Rasles, for whom 'nothing shall be ignored. All shall be included.' Such attitudes Williams considers necessary to the American poet, and he sees Eliot as denying them by the very completeness of his achievement. Eliot is the American poet who has acquired an 'English' detachment, turning to the dead ash of European subject matter, ignoring the new terms that even now must be found for the interpretation and continuation of a New World, and rejecting what Williams came to call the American idiom. Williams was apt to restate his thesis so hastily that it sometimes becomes mere anti-intellectualism, but in its most careful definition it was not so : it embodied a desire that the unknown and unexpressed should not be treated in terms of the already known and expressed.

The desire takes form in Williams's work not as a programme, but as something more important, an exploration. It is true that he was, early on, in sympathy with the Imagists, and he may even have subscribed to Pound's somewhat fuzzily expressed programme for Imagism. But Imagism merely overlapped with the inclinations of Williams himself. He was in love with the bare fact of the external world, its thinginess; and the love mastered him for a lifetime.

In his early poem 'Tract', he rejected the rituals of the past, and he came more and more to realize that his subject-matter lay in the present, and had to be defined without the help of other than what it is. And as much of it had to be defined as possible. 'Nothing shall be ignored. All shall be included.' His love for the external world led him to search for ways of incorporating more and more of it into his poetry. This search is the preoccupation of any good writer, particularly when he is starting to write, and moreover it is fully in accord with an American literary tradition; but for Williams it was the central fact of his poetry, accounting for his greatest successes and worst failures. He was delighted by what he saw at the Armory Show of 1913 :

> I went to it and gaped along with the rest at a 'picture' in which an electric bulb kept going on and off; at Duchamp's sculpture

(by 'Mott and Co.'), a magnificent cast iron urinal, glistening in its white enamel.

In much the same way he was later to include in poems such un-modified 'objects' as the label of a poison-bottle, with skull and crossbones, or a line of Keats. He was to find perfectly proper subject matter in the wallpaper of a room or in a 'lovely ad'. More important, he became increasingly concerned with the attempt to reproduce and re-create the rhythms and language of speech—some-thing we can see he succeeded in doing better than any other poet of the century, if we compare the style of 'The Raper from Passenack' with Pound's curious dialects or the embarrassing pub scene from *The Waste Land.* By so incorporating the things of the New World you can realize a new world of poetry: you become like Boone or Rasles among the Indians of wild Kentucky or Maine.

Such was the emphasis he made, as a writer. We, as readers, may consider that we do not need to make such an emphasis—the acts of exploration and incorporation are made once they are made, and what should continue to interest us is the recorded manner in which they are performed. But performance alone must never be our whole concern. We should be missing nearly everything if we merely noted how quickly he eliminated the exclamatory roman-ticism of his earliest style, and did not also note the romanticism of feeling that remained once that elimination had been made (a feeling Wallace Stevens characterized as 'sentimental'—in a favour-able sense), and that derived from his love, a romantic love, for the subject of his poem.

In such a poem as 'The Red Wheelbarrow', for example, the whole point is in the fact that he has written it, that he has bothered to record with fidelity and economy a phenomenon of the external world. Of the sixteen words in the poem, only the first four, 'So much depends/upon', are suggestive of explanation. And so we have to look into the impulse behind the writing of the poem if we wish to speak about its meaning. Indeed, what 'depends' on such a perception if not everything, man's power to perceive the world? But Williams was not content with writing only this kind of poem. This, and the perhaps even finer 'Poem' of ten years later, describing how a cat jumps over a jamcloset, are legitimate extensions of a particular mode, and perhaps they are more purely Imagist than any of the original works of the Imagists. But as a mode it is limited by the very wideness of its implication, and Williams was aiming at other things as well, in which the technique of description is combined with direct or indirect comment.

'The Red Wheelbarrow' appears in *Spring and All*, a sequence of twenty-eight poems originally mixed with prose when it was published in 1923. In it Williams has reached a full and confident maturity, and a few of the poems must rank among the best in the language. The sureness of direction and the grasp of subject matter seem to result from his decision about the role of the poet, which is defined in the third poem with a firmness in strong contrast to the slight whimsicality of such earlier poems touching the subject as 'Sub Terra' or 'To a Solitary Disciple' or to the later uneasiness of *Paterson*. Here the farmer walking through the rainswept fields in March, meditating on 'the harvest already planted', is seen explicitly as the artist composing. He is also called an 'antagonist' (a word to be taken in both senses, I think, since he is both the antagonist in his work of art and the antagonist to disorder). The poet organizes, plants and meditates on what he has planted, 'in deep thought'. In spite of a hint at the organicism of art, a hint that is undeveloped, the poet could as well be from the seventeenth century as from the twentieth.

It is the greater certainty about his role that accounts for the success of Williams's structural experimentation in this sequence. One of his main concerns seems to be with the ways in which you can go beyond Imagism without abandoning its virtues. How do you not only incorporate things on their own terms (as he does with the red wheelbarrow) but also convey what you conceive to be their value? How, in fact, should meaning enter the poem? On the one hand there is Imagism, where (I have suggested) meaning is to be found in the impulse that causes the poem to be written rather than in the words themselves; and on the other there is general statement, where the poet explicitly *tells* us what value the images have for him. Williams was not, as we might expect, opposed to statement: in spite of the Imagist training he was never to forget completely, he was not afraid of reproducing the content as well as the shape of experience, and the reproduction of content usually takes the form of statement. Between image and statement there is, of course, metaphor: he had indeed earlier experimented with the possibilities of the poem as extended metaphor in 'To Waken an Old Lady' and the more complex 'The Widow's Lament in Spring-time', but though these are successful, if rather fragile poems, he had now come to see such direct metaphor as an evasion of the bareness of reality, which is merely itself, without recourse to comparisons.

The most successful resolution to his problem is the title poem, 'Spring and All', which looks at first sight like description and only that, and certainly lacks any element of direct discourse. It is about the appearance of leaves at the beginning of spring. Williams was much preoccupied with the image of buds or leaves on a branch. They grow with that peculiar combination of un-self-aware vitality and vulnerability that he values so much; in many of his poems there are sexual connotations to his descriptions of them, when he speaks of their 'thrust', or of the buds 'erect with desire against the sky', or of the leafless beech-tree that 'seems to glow/of itself/with a soft stript light/of love'. But in this poem the associations are not sexual. Indeed at first sight there seem to be no associations at all: the things in it are subtly and accurately and decisively *there*, and the poem seems to be about them and them only.

> They enter the new world naked,
> cold, uncertain of all
> save that they enter. All about them
> the cold, familiar wind—
>
>
> Now the grass, tomorrow
> the stiff curl of wildcarrot leaf

Yet because of the feeling behind the poem, which is far deeper and more complex than that behind 'The Red Wheelbarrow', and which is here the sum of numerous hints at feeling in the words themselves, one is moved by the appearance of the leaves: any generalizations about the act of self-definition, of entrance into a cold world, are made by oneself after finishing the poem, but one inevitably makes them. A perfect accuracy of description, by means of which the world is both mastered and lived in, becomes thus a moral perception.

Elsewhere in the sequence are poems in which moral perception is explicit, as general statement—in 'At the Ball Game', where it is as frank as in a poem by Matthew Arnold, in 'Horned Purple', where it is overcome and superseded by the images, and in 'To Elsie', where it is used in correlation with the images. The three poems together constitute a fresh incorporation of material for Williams, sociological in kind, each being about a class of people rather than an individual. 'To Elsie' is the most ambitious. It consists of two very long sentences followed by three short ones.

In the first, generalization moves into more and more limited generalization—almost like a camera panning in from all America to New Jersey, to particular types of people in New Jersey, and finally to one type, the 'young slatterns' who are seduced,

> . . . succumbing without
> emotion
> save numbed terror
>
> under some hedge of choke-cherry
> or viburnum—
> which they cannot express

At this momentary point of rest there is both an implicit comparison between the girls and the hedge-plants, which 'cannot express' either, and an implicit contrast, for the hedge-plants have no terror to express. The second sentence starts with a continued limitation of the generalization until we are shown a particular girl, Elsie, the help in Williams's house; but the instance is not to be a culmination of the process, as it at first appears: it is used as the basis for the largest statement of all, for Elsie embodies a truth about the rest of us:

> as if the earth under our feet
> were
> an excrement of some sky
>
> and we degraded prisoners
> destined
> to hunger until we eat filth

26

while the imagination strains
after deer
going by fields of goldenrod in

the stifling heat of September.

The deer and the goldenrod are related to the choke-cherry and viburnum, those things that are complete from lacking consciousness and the needs imposed by even the inarticulate consciousness of an Elsie. Elsie is merely the extreme example of our helplessness in a state where there is 'no one to drive the car', where we are left at the side of the highway at the mercy of ourselves. It is a poem that might have been no more than an exercise in sentimental pessimism, but the generality of feeling that dominates it is securely held down to the ground by guy-ropes of precise statement, which in turn are pegged there by precise images.

After *Spring and All*, Williams published no poetry in book form for some years, but when he did so again in the early 1930s he continued to write poems clearly springing from the same image of the poet as source of control. In 'The Sea Elephant', 'The Bull', 'New England', 'View of a Lake', 'The Raper from Passenack', and 'Fine Work with Pitch and Copper', the only new tendency to be discerned is that he attempts more often to exploit the rhythms of direct speech. In technique these poems and those from *Spring and All* have little to do with the post-Symbolist tradition as developed by Yeats, Stevens, Crane, Eliot or Pound. They make use, as Yvor Winters has pointed out in his discussion of 'Spring and All', of traditional methods alternating with or strengthened by an Imagist discipline. Their distinction is not only in the excellence of the writing, but in the feeling served by such methods, a feeling 'possessive in that place' which Williams opens.

It is later that a change becomes apparent. In spite of its title, the *Collected Later Poems* is chronologically the second of the four collections of Williams's poetry published,[1] and includes his shorter work of the 1940s. Considering it covers only ten years' work, it is surprisingly long; it is also surprisingly dull. The book

[1] The first is *Collected Earlier Poems*, the third the long poem *Paterson*, and the fourth *Pictures from Brueghel and Other Poems*. [Ed.]

contains a small number of fairly good poems, and numerous echoes of earlier successes, but many of them are spoiled by the presence of moralizing personal assertions, and the tone is often rather tired and hurried, possibly because during this period the best of Williams was going into *Paterson*.

Paterson is the long poem on which he started work in the 1930s. It was planned as four books: the fourth was published in 1951, but a fifth—something of an afterthought—came out in 1958. Each Book is divided into three sections. Paterson is a town in New Jersey, but the poem is also about a man called Paterson—the town is to be seen in terms of a man, the man in terms of a town—and it becomes clearer and clearer as it progresses that the man is Williams himself. The intention was that each Book of the poem should treat of a stage in the course of the river that runs through Paterson, and at the same time of the interrelated aspects of life and poetry suggested to Williams by the activity of the river. The ideas were to emerge from the physical things themselves: the repeated slogan of the poem is 'no ideas but in things', and the first lines make a modest enough announcement of what sounds like inductive method:

> To make a start
> out of particulars
> and make them general, rolling
> up the sum, by defective means—

But in the result ideas tend less to exist in or emerge from things than to alternate with them. There is symbolic and even allegorical writing, there is exact description; there are sustained passages of verse, there are isolated half-lines; there are pieces of prose by Williams, and there are extracts (many of them quite long) from old newspapers, documents, and private letters addressed to Williams. In using material from the past, Williams does not repeat the triumph of *In the American Grain*, where he was prepared to take the past on what he saw as its own terms, living through its style so intensely that it becomes for the time being another kind of present. Instead, he has here turned, surprisingly and disappointingly, to the Poundian technique of fragmentary juxtaposition, particularly between the past and the present. The direct influence of the *Cantos* on *Paterson* is very

clear, not only in the structure but even at times in the ideas (talk
of credit, etc.) and in the style (the passage starting 'Without
invention' appears to be a very successful imitation of Pound's
'With usura', for example). And, since the structure is largely thematic, with little assistance from narrative or logical methods, it
is as apparent as in the *Cantos* that there is going to be a good
deal of waste involved, and that what satisfaction we get will be
local rather than from the work as a whole. Williams did print
some of the best passages separately before their inclusion in
Paterson, and reprinted others after, and so in fact we may feel a
certain justification in making our own anthology of extracts, as
we do with the *Cantos*.

In the early Books, the Falls of the river are established as a
symbol of primitive energy. Williams finds the present lacking,
and it is so specifically because language has undergone a 'divorce'
from that energy. The poem is an attempt to examine the ways
in which we are divorced and the ways in which we are still
'married' to it.

Most readers agree that the quality of the writing declines during
the course of the poem, and the common assumption is that it
does so after Book II, but I find the good poetry in greatest concentration in the second section of Book III. The Book as a whole
is entitled 'The Library', and its subject is the relation between
books and life. From the start of the first section there is an intermittent evocation of 'Beautiful thing', first seen as a blossoming
locust tree, and then merging into a girl in a white lace dress,
possibly a bride, and certainly the victim of assault. We may be
helped in identifying her by bearing in mind the prose sentences
at the beginning of Book I: 'Rigor of beauty is the quest. But how
will you find beauty when it is locked in the mind past all remon-
strance?' She is like the budded branch, or the 'blameless beasts',
and she has the

> dazzled half sleepy eyes
> Beautiful thing
> of some trusting animal.

She is the most important aspect of the new world, she is the subject-matter and the language of poetry that are for Williams poetry itself if they can be allowed to live free on their own terms—not locked in, and not raped.

The first twelve pages of the second section are about the workings of Fire. The image is associated with the process of writing:

> They have
> manoeuvred it so that to write
> is a fire and not only of the blood.

Fire is destructive. There is an account of an Indian fire-rite, in 'a place hidden from/affection, women and offspring', where, 'in the tobacco hush', the Indians lie 'huddled (a huddle of books)', books being further interpreted as 'men in hell,/their reign over the living ended'. There follow prose accounts of fires in towns. Fire destroys even Sappho's poems. But fire also transforms:

> An old bottle, mauled by the fire
> gets a new glaze, the glass warped
> to a new distinction, reclaiming the
> undefined.

The fire as it advances, consuming, takes on a power which recalls that of the imagination. It becomes like the Falls of the river, but 'a cataract reversed'. And at times, Beautiful thing is glimpsed through the fire, but it is difficult to know at this point whether she is apart from the flames or of the flames—though she is seen once 'intertwined' with them, suggesting the subject of poetry intertwined with the process of writing, and we are finally told that she is 'the flame's lover'.

Most of the description of the fire's advance is very vivid, but the explanation supplied by the discursive elements is often unclear; partly, I think, because Williams is no longer content with the image of the poet as farmer, and has become genuinely uncertain about the value of his writing, as we can tell from the following rather clumsy lines:

> nothing is so unclear, between man and
> his writing, as to which is the man and
> which the thing and of them both which
> is the more to be valued.

Books are valueless, he goes on to say, if they contain 'nothing of you', 'you' being the writer. But the admonition is so loose that it tells us very little. Finally the fire dies down and we are left among the ruins and the dead, which are apparently the books.

There follows a letter to a woman beginning 'Hi Kid' and signed 'DJB'. It is barely literate, but has the charm of directness. It could be used to exemplify either the poverty of language after its rape or the virtues of the unliterary American idiom. Williams probably intends it to do the latter, but we cannot be certain, because its relationship with what comes before and after is merely that of juxtaposition.

The remaining four pages or so of the section take us from the process of writing to the subject itself. A doctor is visiting Beautiful thing in the basement smelling of 'furnace odor' where she lies, her 'long/body stretched out negligently on the dirty sheet'. The movement of the verse, gentle and hesitant, carries much of the feeling:

>   —for I was overcome
> by amazement and could do nothing but admire
> and lean to care for you in your quietness—
>
> who looked at me, smiling, and we remained
> thus looking, each at the other . in silence .
>
> You lethargic, waiting upon me, waiting for
> the fire and I
>   attendant upon you, shaken by your beauty

She is still in life, not yet intertwined with the fire she is awaiting that will make her into poetry. She is Elsie-like, vulnerable yet strangely powerful in her lack of developed consciousness. There follow images of the tapestry hunt of the unicorn, images which Williams is to resume in Book V, and then the fine passage ('But you!/in your white lace dress') part of which had been printed separately in the 1930s, which shows how Beautiful thing has been misused: she has been given a 'busted nose', and 'maled and femaled . . . jealously'.

And how is he, after all, to bring her into his poetry without destroying her? He must preserve the thing she is by preserving the precarious mixture of reverence and tenderness that he feels for her: and if writing is like a fire then the fire he brings to brighten her corner must be different from the other, it must be neither destructive nor transforming, it must be 'a dark flame'.

The whole four pages are as good as anything in *Paterson*, and go far to redeem the frequent messiness of the poem elsewhere. Williams is more unsure than he was in *Spring and All* about the relation between life and its transformation (or destruction) in writing, and his unsureness shows at times in the unclear connections between the description of the fire and the meanings attributed to it, in spite of the power of much of that description. But in this last part it is his very unsureness that is the subject of his writing, while his style takes on assurance. The tentative formation of relationship between doctor and patient, or between lover and lover, becomes the relationship between writer and subject in the process of realization; and the contrasting passage that follows, about the savaging of Beautiful thing, in its account of the denial of that process, is equally moving and equally assured.

It was Eliot who dominated poetry until the early 1950s, and such is literary fashion that apparently Williams could not but suffer— being misunderstood or, more commonly, disregarded under such dominance. By all the critics who followed Eliot's lead (that is, by most critics), Williams was regarded, when he was remembered, as a kind of Menshevik, without importance. His work was unpublished and thus largely unread in England until after his death, and less than ten years ago an influential English critic could still sum it up as 'William Carlos Williams' poetry of red brick houses, suburban wives, cheerful standardised interiors'. America is larger than England, and thus has a little more room for variety, but there too literary opinion is centralized, and in that huge landscape Williams often went undiscerned in the 1930s and 1940s.

What must be stressed, at this late date, is that he offers a valid alternative of style and attitude to the others available. It is offered not in his theory, which is fragmentary, sometimes inconsistent, and often poorly expressed, but in his poetry, which is among the best of our time. He is somebody from whom it is time we started taking lessons. Although he insisted on the American idiom, we must remember why: writing 'thoroughly local in origin has some chance of being universal in application'; that idiom is part of a widely-used language, his enrichment of which has a bearing on all of us who read it and write it.

The first book of his to be published over here[1] was his most recently written, *Pictures from Brueghel*, which contains his last three collections of poems. There is a bareness about it that I can imagine was at first disconcerting to readers unfamiliar with Williams. But the bareness is not a sign of tiredness, rather it is the translation into language of a new ease in his relationship with the external world. A result of the ease is seen in the much greater emphasis on the personal that we find in this volume. In 'Dog Injured in the Street' and 'The Drunk and the Sailor', for example, poems which twenty years before would merely have implied Williams as onlooker, the subject is Williams himself so much involved in what he witnesses that he as good as participates in it. Another result of the ease is in the style, which is transparent to his intentions as never before. Statement emerges from Williams as both subject and author of the poem, not from him merely as author.

It is, however, from *Paterson* that Williams consciously dates his final development in style. The passage from Book II that he here reprints as a separate poem entitled 'The Descent' contains many lines divided into three parts, which he called 'variable feet'. I do not find the name very clear: as Alan Stephens has pointed out in a review, a variable foot is as meaningless a term as an elastic inch; but if calling it so helped Williams to write this last volume, then it is sufficiently justified. Specifically, it gave him a rationale for the short lines grouped in threes that he wanted to use, of which the rhythms are as flexible and varied as in the best of his earlier poetry. This poem is about old age and is expressed largely in abstract terms; in tone, even in sound, it bears an astonishing—though we may hardly assume derivative—resemblance to some of the best passages of the *Four Quartets*: it advances with a halting, exploratory movement which is itself much of the poem's meaning. He is speaking of the re-creation achieved by memory:

[1] i.e. in England, where this essay was written. The other pieces in this book were written in California. [Ed.]

No defeat is made up entirely of defeat—since
the world it opens is always a place
           formerly
                  unsuspected. A
world lost,
     a world unsuspected,
              beckons to new places
and no whiteness (lost) is so white as the memory
              of whiteness.

Memory is a means of renewal, and for Williams anything that renews is an instrument for the exploration and definition of the new world, which he labours both to 'possess' and be part of. For possession of the details is achieved not through the recording of them, but through the record's adherence to his feeling for them. The process is not of accumulation but of self-renewal.

> The roar of the present, a speech
> is, of necessity, my sole concern

he has said, in *Paterson*, but he is agent for the present only through the fidelity of his love for it.

The nature of the process is defined in this book with a renewed confidence, also. If in *Spring and All* the poet is seen as the firm antagonist to disorder and in *Paterson* as helplessly involved with that disorder, he is seen in 'The Sparrow' finally as in a world where perhaps the words' order and disorder are irrelevant. The sparrow is to a certain degree helpless, but he can 'flutter his wings/in the dust' and 'cry out lustily'. In this poem the poet and his subject-matter share in the same activity, the essence of which is the expression of delight at one's own vigour. Vigour and delight inform the style itself, relating anecdote, description and statement smoothly and easily. 'It is the poem/of his existence/that triumphed/finally', he says of the sparrow, and in saying so might have been writing his own epitaph, for poem and existence are seen here to be expressed in similar terms.

There is more than self-expression involved; and, clearly, if we wish to learn from Williams's achievement, we should mark the clarity of evocation, the sensitivity of movement, and the purity of language in his efforts to realize spontaneity. But at the same time we should remember that these qualities, easy as they are to localize, cannot be learned from him in isolation. They, and the self-discipline controlling them, derive from a habitual sympathy, by which he recognizes his own energy in that of the young house-wife, the boys at the street corner, the half-wit girl who helps in the house, the sparrow, or the buds alternating down a bough. His stylistic qualities are governed, moreover, by a tenderness and generosity of feeling which make them fully humane. For it is a humane action to attempt the rendering of a thing, person, or experience in the exact terms of its existence.

THE EARLY SNYDER

1. INTERPENETRATING THINGS

A Range of Poems, by Gary Snyder, Fulcrum Press.

> His hat was made of birch bark, his clothes were ragged and worn out, and his shoes were wood. Thus men who have made it hide their tracks: unifying categories and interpenetrating things.
>
> Snyder's translation of the Preface to the Poems of Han-Shan

This book contains Gary Snyder's complete short poems, including his latest collection, *The Back Country*, and a group of translations from the Japanese poet Miyazawa Kenji, neither of which has yet been published in the USA. Fifteen years ago, the English hardly credited North America with having any poetry at all; but they are now, it turns out, ready to accept all and any American poetry. I find this great cause for cheerfulness: better, always, to accept too much than too little. And, since this is a collection of a very good and very important young poet, I want in this article to do more than merely rejoice, I want to be specific about Snyder's qualities.

The best place to start with him has always been with the first poem of his first published book, since it is still one of the best he has written, it is immediately attractive, and it shows a certain basic attitude of his at its simplest.

GARY SNYDER

Mid-August at Sourdough Mountain Lookout

Down valley a smoke haze
Three days heat, after five days rain
Pitch glows on the fir-cones
Across rocks and meadows
Swarms of new flies.

I cannot remember things I once read
A few friends, but they are in cities.
Drinking cold snow-water from a tin cup
Looking down for miles
Through high still air.

It is a poem about feeling the cleanness of the senses, and cleanness, exactness, adequacy are the first impressions we have of the language and the rhythms. There is neither regret nor complacency in the poem : what he does not have he does not have, but what he does have—up here alone in a fire lookout—is an intense clarity of sensation, like a gift. It is a poem of fact, not of metaphor or symbol; statement does all the work, and we are invited to test it by only the most general of human experiences, a knowledge of what it feels like to be up a mountain, for instance, or of what water tastes like. The general invitation into the specific experience is most characteristic of Snyder's art, for the whole gist is that what we can share is likely to be *as such* valuable. And the rhythms, at one with the perceptions, neither their servants nor their masters, are a sufficient commentary on the adequacy of the things experienced in the last three lines of the poem.

His antecedents are obvious enough, and his early poetry is perfectly open in acknowledging them. There are one or two poems where he tries rather unsuccessfully to work with the denunciatory tone of the long Ginsbergian line; there is another, 'The Stone Garden', where he experiments with the iambic line in a surprisingly dull meditation; a more congenial influence is Rexroth, whose manner of disposing details briefly shows up in 'Kyoto : March', but the influence is quickly absorbed. Towering behind stand Pound and Williams. Snyder has learned from them not only a lot about verse-rhythms but what creates those rhythms—a habit of accurate observation which imposes on the observer a humility before the world.

He is closest to Williams when he writes of the personal perceptions made from the middle of work or of love: they are not
special, Donne-like or Yeats-like perceptions, but those of a modest
and honest man entrusting himself to his experience. He is closest
to Pound not only in his use of the 'ideogrammic' line but in his
interest in fertility magic: often in Snyder, as in the Pound of
Canto 47, we find the rituals of the life-cycle presented without
pedantry or patronage, rather with a simple fidelity in the recording,
which is the equivalent to participation.

Here, though, I have already started to define what makes Snyder
distinct from Williams and Pound. You start by learning from
masters, but if you are talented enough, the difference in your own
circumstances and your own preoccupations are going to start taking
over from the masters, and bit by bit your own world is going to
be raised. Bit by bit Snyder's own world is raised in this book. His
circumstances are not those of Williams—he is not a New Jersey
doctor but a man of many jobs, who has been among other things
a merchant seaman, a logger, a university teacher, and a student
in a Buddhist monastery: such jobs start at once to impose their
own rhythms on Snyder's attitudes. (He has said: 'the rhythms of
my poems follow the rhythm of the physical work I'm doing and
life I'm leading at any given time.') And his preoccupations are
different from Pound's—the interest in Buddhism is I think less
didactic, the interest in magic is in that of the American Indians.

The circumstances and (though indirectly) the preoccupations
show up in the following poem, which is about getting another drink
of water.

The Spring

Beating asphalt into highway potholes
      pickup truck we'd loaded
road repair stock shed & yard
a day so hot the asphalt went in soft.
      pipe and steel plate temper
took turns at by hand
then drive the truck rear wheel
a few times back and forth across the fill—
finish it off with bitchmo round the edge.

           the foreman said let's get a drink
        & drove through woods and flower fields
              shovels clattering in back
        into a black grove by a cliff
              a rocked in pool
              feeding a fern ravine
                    tin can to drink
        numbing the hand and cramping in the gut
        surging thru the fingers from below
              & *dark here*—
        let's get back to the truck
        get back on the job.

The lines of the first section are far more abruptly separated than
the lines of the other poem. They do something Snyder is fond
of—a naming of the tools and processes of a job, dryly, factually,
using the terms of the workmen. It recalls the start of another,
earlier poem, 'Hay for the Horses', and as in that one—though the
jostle of inflexible terms seems at first sight to be all there is, items,
the routine, the fact of the job being all there is time for—the
personal observation enters among them. The abrupt hard rhythms,
the almost unconnected words, the clustering consonants are modi-
fied by the human (here, the iambic) rhythm of the man noticing
that the heat is so great that 'the asphalt went in soft'. And it is
this that, very modestly, localizes the job as Snyder's and brings
him as the speaker into the poem. The second section is a contrast
that emerges out of the clatter of the first, the continuity being made
specifically by 'shovels clattering in back'. But it does contrast in
subject and in movement, though it is like in that it continues to
name things rather than dwelling on them with the detail of Keats
or Hart Crane. They are named yet sufficiently presented: and so
in this bare context a word like 'feeding' has a very big impact,
implying the dependence of the ferns on the pool, the easy inter-
connected uninterruptedness of the life the two men have chanced
on. 'Surging' also implies a lot, the quiet surprising strength of the
water, a very different water from his drink on Sourdough Mountain.
So when we reach them we are wholly able to interpret the italics
of '& *dark here*—': it is desire-plus-terror as you get a hint of the
silent powerful and leisurely purposefulness of the large and un-

known, before you hurry back to the job, and really hurrying back too, with more hurry than is called for by the job alone.

Snyder's verse, its look on the page, may well remind us of other poems, by writers out of San Francisco or associated with Black Mountain College. In it conventional punctuation is at a minimum, and the syntax is mostly paratactic, i.e. there is little subordination, and the phrase is the important structural unit. The comparative looseness of the form is very attractive, and because the rhythms may constantly vary the verse is hospitable to many elements that metrical and accentual and certain kinds of free verse can seldom digest—bits of experience, for example fragments of speech heard, bits of notices seen on walls. The dangers of proceeding from phrase to phrase, however, are not to be sniffed at; for a poem written thus may be so loosely structured, so relaxed, that it will be diffuse and dull as a whole (something I find about most of Charles Olson's poetry, even though I am aware how much Olson's example and precepts have taught poets I admire). Some of Snyder's longer poems, especially some of those not included in this volume, published in San Francisco as *Six Sections from Mountains and Rivers Without End*, tend to fall to pieces in this way : 'Night Highway Ninety-Nine', for instance, is really only a list of vivid details with nothing to hold them together but Snyder's knowledge that they did in fact occur to him in something like the recorded sequence. His strength is still greatest in the short poem.

Snyder's first book is called *Riprap*, which is defined on the title page as 'a cobble of stone laid on steep slick rock to make a trail for horses in the mountains'. And there is a further gloss elsewhere when he speaks of 'Poetry a riprap on the slick rock of metaphysics'. The poem is a trail which offers a secure foothold where metaphysics doesn't. But in committing ourselves to poem as to metaphysics we are still trying to get from one point to another, the direction is still the same, we are trying to relate the things of experience to each other in a general effort to evaluate them. How he does the relating and evaluating is how he structures the poem, and this is difficult to generalize about, since his practice varies anywhere between the traditional poem ending with the generalization which sums up, e.g. 'Hop, Skip, and Jump', and the poem of thematic juxtaposition, e.g. 'Bubbs Creek Haircut' (which seems to me the most successful of the extracts from *Mountains and Rivers Without End*). In either case his hold over the structure is both firm and sensitive, so that the poem never in any of its parts goes dead on him, there is never the relaxation, the diffusion I have mentioned as a danger. One of the loveliest of the poems new to me in this book is 'The Manichaeans', which shows the two structural techniques combined. The poem is about two lovers in bed, but much of the imagery seems at first to have only an indirect bearing on them. Parts of the poem light up and go out in turn, like lights on a pinball machine:

> Cable-car cables
> Whip over their greast rollers
> Two feet underground.
> > hemmed in by mysteries
> > all moving in order.

Then at the end the whole poem lights up:

> We shall sing in this heat
> > of our arms
> Blankets like rock-strata fold
> > dreaming as
> > > Shiva and Shakti
> And keep back the cold.

The two lovers are seen not only in their warm tiny individuality, surrounded by disparate things, but now, in their attempt to 'keep back the cold', as god and goddess, universal principles of male and female. The variety of images we have experienced in turn through the poem now light up together in retrospect as we come to the last three lines.

Not only are the poems carefully and sensitively structured, they are kept alive at every point by the rhythms and the language. The stressed and unstressed syllables are quite sharply distinguishable and group easily into tight clear rhythmic units. And the qualities of the rhythms are closely connected with those of the language. His poetry is full of things caught in motion: as the ghost logger walks, 'berry-brambles catch at the stagged pants'; on the coast 'mussels clamp to sea-boulders/Sucking the spring tides'; a deer runs with 'stiff springy jumps down the snowfields/Head held back, forefeet out,/Balls tight in a tough hair sack'; the father in the public bath washes his daughters, he 'soaps up and washes their/ plump little tight-lip pussies/peers in their ears'. I emphasize the motion because Snyder has few still-lifes: his poetry is in constant motion because the things he is speaking about are in constant motion, thus the verse movement and the words interpret each other.

Life brushes up against him as, in Pound,

> Sniff and pad-foot of beasts,
>   fur brushing my knee-skin.

But it does not do this unless you let it: Snyder has worked to lay himself open to the feel, look, sound and smell of things. Attentiveness becomes in him as it does in Williams a form of moral discipline. The act of attentiveness is, too, one in which you can fully live, and its analogues are to be found in the deer running, the mussels sucking, the man and woman making love, and the labourer at his job. These acts are a means of 'unifying categories and interpenetrating things'.

2. WAKING WITH WONDER

The Back Country, by Gary Snyder, Fulcrum Press.

Six Sections from Mountains and Rivers Without End, by Gary Snyder, Fulcrum Press.

M. L. Rosenthal in his handbook *The New Poets* devoted only one-third of a sentence to the work of Gary Snyder, something I found a bit surprising, since Snyder is clearly one of the best half-a-dozen poets of the generation Rosenthal was talking about. The reason for the near-omission is that he was so interested in grouping poets into schools and movements that he found it difficult to perceive talent existing outside them. The mistake is common, but it is still a shameful one, since most real talent cannot be so classified and thus it gets overlooked. Snyder is ungroupable: he is more concrete and sensuous than the Black Mountain poets; he is more concise and less loosely visionary than the Beat poets; he lacks the rather arch surrealism of the Bly school; he does not boast about experience in hospitals and mental institutions, so he is not a

Confessional; and he certainly cannot be said to fall into another of Mr Rosenthal's favourite categories, that of Irish poets. Of course, one cannot expect that Snyder himself should be interested in this business of literary classification. He does the real thing, after all, he writes poetry, and like most serious poets he is mainly concerned at finding himself on a barely known planet in an almost unknown universe, where he must attempt to create and discover meanings.

Discovery of a meaning is always also the creation of it, and creation is an act of discovery. The way Snyder sets about the double process can be seen at its clearest in many of his shortest poems, from the first in his first book, *Riprap*, to a number of the poems in his latest, *The Back Country* (which is a greatly expanded version of the last section of the collected poems published by Fulcrum Press as *A Range of Poems*). A good example is 'North Beach Alba':

> waking half-drunk in a strange pad
> making it out to the cool gray
>   san francisco dawn—
> white gulls over white houses,
>   fog down the bay,
> tamalpais a fresh green hill in the new sun,
> driving across the bridge in a beat old car
>   to work.

This is the whole poem. Like Williams's 'The Red Wheelbarrow', it is deceptively simple. It is as important for what it leaves out as for what it includes, and for the economy in which the perceptions overtake each other and accrete. For it is not a picture, but a series of pictorial perceptions made by a man embedded in time, who advances into the sensory world opened by his waking. At first sight, it might seem a limited kind of poetry, but no poetry that engages us so fully in our own world could be called limited. The crisp bare presentation carries its own implication of values. The 'cool gray' of the early morning, where energy is in abeyance, is succeeded by the image of Mount Tamalpais (visible from North Beach in San Francisco and from the Golden Gate Bridge), suggesting energy as a potential and close at hand. It is 'fresh . . . in the new sun'. And all of Snyder's world is fresh and new—the word applies both to his style and his subject-matter. Again and again the experience of awaking occurs in his poetry; and he wakes with a sensation of wonder into a place filling up with light.

His poetry is 'personal', in that it is almost all written in the first person, but, as I have said, he could never be called a 'confessional' poet. There is a great contrast between the modesty and economy of his 'To Hell with your Fertility Cult', for example, and the verbose agonizings that certain confessional poets would conduct over the subject, a quarrel between a man and woman that is exploding into an act of physical and almost comic violence. Interestingly, this poem is one of the comparatively few written in the third person. And its modesty comes from the fact that he is interested not in the unique experience but in the shared or sharable experience, the successive awakenings to wonder, to awareness and to sympathy.

Indeed, the shared experience in Snyder's poetry is a kind of simultaneous waking on the part of more than one person. He speaks of how, on a walking tour fifteen years back, he and his first wife met a boy who was a look-out on a mountain, and ends:

> I don't know where she is now;
> I never asked your name.
> In this burning, muddy, lying,
> blood-drenched world
> that quiet meeting in the mountains
> cool and gentle as the muzzles of
> three elk, helps keep me sane.

The rather general and rhetorical third and fourth lines are not particularly characteristic of Snyder, but the image that succeeds them (to cancel them) is: both in its precise and unrhetorical style and in its subject. The image resolves the poem, in a sense *is* the poem. For Snyder perceives and communicates largely in images (though there are exceptional poems where he does not—for example, the very successful, almost Creeley-like 'Across Lamarck Col'). His danger is not that of most of us, that we might generalize the world away, but that the accidental world itself might take over the poem. There were some poems of his in *Poetry* some time ago, which he does not republish here, lists of 'things to do in San Francisco', 'things to do on a ship', which were no more than that, simply lists. As it is, there are in *The Back Country* a poem called 'How to Make Stew in the Pinacate Desert', a poem containing lists of English words to be learned by Japanese students, and another listing chores done around the house. But there can be no

question that these last three *are* poems—the recipe and the lists
are embodied in a context of human activity, and one way of
pointing to Snyder's special virtues would be to sum up the differences between, say, the bare recipe and the poem that contains it.

The structure of most of the longer poems could be described as
based on the Poundian method of juxtaposed images, which is a
method of putting all the weight on clarity and vividness of detail.
In the *Six Sections from Mountains and Rivers Without End*, I don't
think it comes off. The connections seem very loose, both within
sections and between sections, and most of the detail lacks the
firmness and clarity of Snyder's best writing. It is in the middle-
length poems in *The Back Country* that the method is used with
such variety and inventiveness. 'The Old Dutch Woman', for
example, is about contemplators in gardens: it ends with an extraordinary image comparing greenfly on rose-leaves to distant mountain goats picking their way over snow. The close implies the far.
Something similar is happening in the much more complex 'The
Manichaeans', where the tininess of the lovers on their bed eventually becomes their enormousness as they sum up the universe.
In 'For the West', the images are tied together linguistically: in
rather the same way as he puns on the word 'goodwill' in 'Bubbs
Creek Haircut', he here puns on the word 'revolution' as an inevitable process like the revolutions or turnings of the world. He starts
the poem speaking of Europe, but towards the end remarks:

> Ah, that's America:
> the flowery glistening oil blossom
>   spreading on water—
> it was so tiny, nothing, now it keeps expanding
> all those colors,
>   our world
>   opening inside outward toward us,
> each part swelling and turning
> who would have thought such turning;
> as it covers,
>   the colors fade,
> and the fantastic patterns
>   fade.
> I see down again through clear water.

The image is almost dream-like in its shiftings, but it is performing something of the same function as conceptual language, for it is an image for the history of America.

Here and elsewhere in *The Back Country* the language is consistently powerful, it is cool and exact, with no ambitions toward a grand style to intrude between him and his perceptions. He patiently records the world, as an act of love, with all his senses opened to it. His work is, after all, a poetry of feeling, feeling exquisitely defined by its objects.

FULKE GREVILLE

I *Life and Works*

There is not a great deal to say about Fulke Greville's life, which
was for the most part that of a highly placed civil servant. He was
born in 1554 in Warwickshire, where his father was a big land-
owner. From childhood he and Philip Sidney were close friends :
they came to court together, and both prepared for a life of public
service in diplomacy, administration, and war. Greville was much
valued by the Queen, as may be inferred from her preventing him
from going abroad as much as he wanted : more than once, on his
way to the continent, he was stopped at ports by her orders and so
had to return to court.

Greville shared with Sidney an interest in Calvinism, which was
also a political interest in that century when 'religious opinion was,
far more often than not, political opinion also.'[1] It is important to
remember, though, that their Calvinism was not that brand of
Puritan thought which challenged the authority of the monarch.

They also shared a devotion to the art of poetry. Sidney was a
kind of sixteenth-century Ezra Pound, the most influential poet and
critic of his time; and Greville, his closest friend, was obviously the
first to be caught up in his experimental excitement : it is likely
indeed that they would sometimes write on chosen themes in
conscious rivalry.[2] As a result of Sidney's influence, fame and

[1] J. W. Allen, *A History of Political Thought in the Sixteenth Century*,
London, 1928, p. 78.
[2] This is suggested by John Buxton in *Sir Philip Sidney and the English
Renaissance*, London, 1954.

example, Wilton, the country house of his sister, the Countess of Pembroke, became a centre of patronage. And not only his friends Greville and Dyer, but Spenser, countless sonneteers who never knew him personally, and a whole decade of pastoral poets in the 1590s, fed on Sidney's example and were more influenced by him than by any other writer.

Sidney's death in 1586 was the most deeply affecting event in Greville's life. He wanted to go with Leicester into the Low Countries and fight where Sidney had died, but Elizabeth refused to let him, having already lost one valued servant. He resisted her at first, but finally gave way:

> I finding the specious fires of youth to prove far more scorching than glorious, called my second thoughts to counsel, and in that map clearly discerning action and honour, to fly with more wings than one: and that it was sufficient for the plant to grow where his sovereign's hand had placed it; I found reason to contract my thoughts from these larger, but wandering horizons, of the world abroad, and to bound my prospect within the safe limits of duty, in such home services, as were acceptable to my sovereign.[1]

Thereafter he worked at court for Elizabeth, holding increasingly important positions. He withdrew for a few years on her death, but returned to work for James I and then Charles I. In 1621 he was made Lord Brooke, and by the time of his death had become one of the richest men in the country. In 1628 he was stabbed and killed by an old servant who believed he had not been provided for in his will. Greville himself composed the epitaph which was inscribed on the monument to him in a church in Warwick: 'Servant to Queen Elizabeth, Councillor to King James, Friend to Sir Philip Sidney'.

Except for a few poems from *Caelica* and a pirated edition of one of his plays, none of Greville's writings appeared during his lifetime. As a result, there is no certainty about the dates of his works. However, their order of composition can be conjectured.

Caelica, the collection of his short poems, must come earliest.

---

[1] Greville, *Life of Sidney*.

Bullough[1] believes that the poems were started between 1577 and 1580 and that they were all, or almost all, written by 1600. Moreover, he considers that they are arranged in a roughly chronological order, a belief which is supported by considerations of style and subject-matter.

It is perhaps unfortunate that Greville's best-known poem in modern times has been 'O wearisome condition of humanity', since it is a chorus from one of the plays, and anyone who likes it well enough to read more of him would probably turn first to that play and be rather bored. Greville wrote two plays, *Mustapha* and *Alaham*, though he tells us of another, about Antony and Cleopatra, which he destroyed on the fall of Essex, for fear of misinterpretation. His object in the plays was 'to trace out the high ways of ambitious governors'. They are deliberately closet dramas, in which there is no attempt at character delineation or control of dramatic pace; they are in fact virtually long poems divided into scenes consisting of lengthy rhetorical speeches exchanged by the characters.

We know that the treatises, or long poems, on *Humane Learning*, *Fame and Honour*, *Wars*, *Monarchy*, and *Religion*, followed the plays, growing out of them, since they 'were first intended to be for every act a chorus'. They are often swifter-moving than the plays, for Greville is now no longer impeded by what was for him the mere artifice of dramatic convention, but they are extremely uneven in the writing. For stretches they are stylistically merely versified essays, though there are passages of great power alternating with much that is lame and verbose. They do not have the consistent rhetorical power and cunning of Dryden's didactic poems; like Greville's plays, they are of greater historical than literary interest. U. M. Ellis Fermor's is the best comment on them:

> Much of his speculative poetry is an undergrowth of statement, inference, reference and deduction, contradicting and balancing each other, until no conclusion is free from its corresponding doubt, no imaginative experience complete and clear. . . . Through long passages in these poems . . . he seems to lay a generous foundation for his interpretation of human destiny and then, unable to comprehend the elements he has

[1] Geoffrey Bullough, editor of *Poems and Dramas of Fulke Greville, First Lord Brooke*, Edinburgh, 1939. [Ed.]

assembled, to go astray among them, to be saved from pedantic frivolity only by a certain weary magnificence of intention persisting in a task beyond its strength.[1]

Lastly there is the *Life of Sidney*, a long prose work intended as dedication to Greville's collected works that were never published during his lifetime. It is both more and less than a life of his friend, which occupies only the first two-thirds of the work, the remainder being largely a political essay with some interesting autobiographical detail.

II *Literary Background*

Greville came of age at a time when English poetry was already vigorous, self-conscious and mature. Rumours to the contrary have no doubt been caused by the literary historians who pay much attention to a popular work like *A Mirror for Magistrates* and little to the contemporary collections of short poems. The first usefully illustrates orthodox Elizabethan political thought but is crudely written and dull; the others tell us comparatively little about such things but sometimes contain poetry of great strength. Predominant among the best poets before Sidney and Greville were Sir Thomas Wyatt, whose poems were not widely circulated until the publication of Tottel's miscellany in 1557, and George Gascoigne, whose poems were published in 1573 and 1575. There was also a large body of impressive anonymous poetry, mainly songs and ballads, which had a direct and clear influence on the later Elizabethans.

The ruling style before Sidney has been called native, plain and drab, depending on whether the describer has liked or disliked it. Characteristically it is based on statement (rather than metaphor), often compressed into *sententiae*, which were sometimes printed in italics. At its worst, the effect is of plodding metrical prose—the statements are pompously didactic, the *sententiae* are only too easily separable from their contexts, the device of alliteration becomes heavy, and the rhythms are monotonous and unvaried. At its best, it has a compactness in which alliteration becomes a grace

---

[1] U. M. Ellis Fermor, Introduction, *Caelica*. This modernization of *Caelica* appeared as a limited edition brought out by the Greynog Press, Montgomeryshire, in 1939, and I do not believe the useful Introduction has since been reprinted.

like the grace of rhyme, and in which the movement is emphatic
without becoming deadening; and the straightforwardness of
language and device is the very medium through which energy of
thought and feeling emerges. In Gascoigne the style can take on
great power. Here is an example where, speaking in the third person,
he describes how he gave up trying to be a courtier to become a
soldier:

> But now behold what mark the man doth find:
> He shoots to be a soldier in his age;
> Mistrusting all the virtues of the mind,
> He trusts the power of his personage,
> As though long limbs led by a lusty heart
> Might yet suffice to make him rich again;
> But flushing frays have taught him such a part
> That now he thinks the wars yield no such gain.
> And sure I fear, unless your lordship deign,
> To train him yet into some better trade,
> It will be long before he hit the vein,
> Whereby he may a richer man be made.
> He cannot climb as other catchers can,
> To lead a charge before himself be led;
> He cannot spoil the simple sakeless man
> Which is content to feed him with his bread;
> He cannot pinch the painful soldier's pay
> And shear him out his share in ragged sheets;
> He cannot stop to take a greedy prey
> Upon his fellows grovelling in the streets;
> He cannot pull the spoil from such as pill,
> And seem full angry at such foul offence,
> Although the gain content his greedy will
> Under the cloak of contrary pretence.
>
> ('Gascoigne's Woodmanship')

Yvor Winters has distinguished between two kinds of plain style
among the Elizabethans—the aphoristic and the expository.[1]
Clearly this passage is expository, but its derivation from the
aphorism is noticeable: a line like 'He cannot climb as other

[1] Yvor Winters, 'The 16th Century Lyric in England', *Poetry*, February,
March and April 1939. This section of my essay owes a good deal to his
article.

catchers can' has both the generalizing force and the alliterative manner of the aphorism. But it is more than aphorism, in that it cannot be separated from its context. Its succinctness and directness only serve to make clearer the complexity of Gascoigne's attitude to his experience. He cannot help regretting his failure, but at the same time his regret is tempered by his knowledge of the brutality and unscrupulousness of those who 'succeed' as soldiers. The writing contains a lot of general moral comment, but it is completely saved from mere didacticism by the sensitive fluctuation of the tone from one of vigorous self-criticism to one of unpretentious humanity. Both in the extract and in the poem as a whole the larger implications are constantly related to his personal feelings and actions, and exist only in that relationship.

Gascoigne's remarks about poetry are more naive than his practice. In his *Certain Notes of Instruction* he speaks of 'invention' as 'the first and most necessary' element of poetry. What he means by invention is made clear from the following passage :

> If I should disclose my pretence in love, I would either make a strange discourse of some intolerable passion, or find occasion to plead by the example of some history, or discover my disquiet in shadows *per Allegoriam*, or use the covertest mean that I could to avoid the uncomely customs of common writers.

He means something very simple : inventiveness, we would say, or ingenuity, so as to persuade or even trick the reader into accepting what one says by one's attractive indirection. It is remarkable, however, that Gascoigne in practice is direct and muscular, and that there is seldom to be found in his poetry that excess of ornamentation which is the vice often resulting from over-ingenuity. 'Invention' as he actually uses it in his 'Lullaby' or 'Woodmanship' is a mastering or organizing rather than a local or incidental device : in the one he uses the form of a lullaby to sing his youth, his 'gazing eyes', his will, and 'Robin' to sleep; in the other he uses the metaphor of the hunt, where his missing the deer with his arrows symbolizes his past failures, his missing of chances.

But in his precept of elaboration and indirection, he looks forward to the most famous development in Elizabethan poetry, that initiated by Sidney. Many poets suffered—and continued to suffer, well into the next century—from a puzzled sense of national inferiority to the classical and Italian poets. Sidney enquires in his *Apology* 'why

England (the mother of excellent minds) should be grown so hard a stepmother to poets'. Sidney and his friends therefore made a conscious attempt to extend the range of English poetry by exercising it in as many ways as possible, exploring new metres and verse-forms, enlarging its vocabulary, and imitating foreign models. In particular, Sidney was at pains to anglicize the Petrarchan sonnet (which Wyatt had already introduced into the country) in his *Astrophel and Stella*, and the Ariostian epic, of which the *Arcadia* was intended as a prose equivalent. The result of his efforts was an emphasis, in many of his poems and in the poems of writers influenced by him, not only on elaborate mastering devices but also on local inventiveness, which often took the form of ornate imagery.

Without these deliberate attempts at sophistication, such writing as the famous sonnet on the moon would have been almost unthinkable:

> With how sad steps, O Moon, thou climb'st the skies!
> How silently, and with how wan a face!
> What, may it be that even in heavenly place
> That busy archer his sharp arrows tries?
> Sure, if that long-with-love-acquainted eyes
> Can judge of love, thou feel'st a lover's case:
> I read it in thy looks: thy languish'd grace,
> To me that feel the like, thy state descries.
> Then even of fellowship, O Moon, tell me,
> Is constant love deem'd there but want of wit?
> Are beauties there as proud as here they be?
> Do they above love to be lov'd, and yet
> Those lovers scorn whom that love doth possess?
> Do they call virtue there ungratefulness?
>
> (*Astrophel and Stella*, XXXI)

It starts with the halting regretful movement of Sidney's perception (the first line would have a different effect if it read 'O Moon, with how sad steps thou climb'st the skies'), and then quickens slightly as he forms the conceit of the third and fourth lines. The resemblance between the moon and the lover is a lot more tenuous than the resemblance Gascoigne found between missing deer and missing chances, for Sidney's comparison depends entirely on the fact that the moon is slow in its movement, and therefore seems sad, like a sad lover. Yet once this resemblance is granted it works surely and

aptly, since Sidney uses it tactfully and never presses it into absurdity: the earthly lover is compared to those 'above' or 'there'
rather than to the moon itself, and thus we are not tempted to take
the comparison so literally that we ask awkward questions like 'Who
is the moon in love with?' Moreover the verse movement continues
to be fully alive at every point, and the four questions at the end
are delivered with all the variety of rhetoric at Sidney's command,
rising to the impatience of the third in which the speaker is so
obsessed with love that he uses the word four times in two lines,
and sinking to the more desperate tone of the simpler and more
personally felt last line.

On the other hand, though the new kind of elaboration is in this
poem magnificently justified, such a poem as *Astrophel and Stella*
XCIX shows the vices of an overdependence on ornament, ornament
here that does not inform the poem as a whole but is strictly local,
and is not even doing its local job well. The lover describes how he
lies awake, 'viewing the shape of darkness', in the first eight lines,
which are clear and strong. The sonnet ends:

> But when birds charm and that sweet air which is
> Morn's messenger with rose-enamell'd skies
> Calls each wight to salute the flower of bliss,
> In tombs of lids then buried are mine eyes,
> Forc'd by their lord, who is asham'd to find
> Such light in sense with such a darken'd mind.

A simple thought is here being dressed up in clothes of a rather
tawdry richness. Clearly there were losses as well as gains in having
advanced beyond the plain style. Not only are the words imprecisely
and tritely decorative (charm, sweet, rose-enamell'd), but there is a
tendency to ridiculous circumlocution, as in the fourth line quoted,
and Sidney is led into damaging vagueness in at least two phrases
suggesting deliquescent conceits: we shall never know exactly
what the flower of bliss may be, and is the lord of the eyes merely
Sidney himself, or his mind, or someone not mentioned in the
poem—the god of love, perhaps?

There were thus two styles available—the plain and the ornate.
There was to be, of course, a third stage of elaboration, in the metaphysical image. It was already latent in the Petrarchan conceit: given
the conceit, and given the interest in ingenuity, it was inevitable.
One of the fascinating things about reading Shakespeare's sonnets and

early plays is to find him often hovering in that area between the conceit and the metaphysical image where a figure is so far elaborated that it is no longer simply the one but not so far elaborated that it can be called the other. Certainly the metaphysical image would have emerged without Donne, and it is possible that it did emerge before him, but it was left to Donne to develop it with such ruthless consistency that at times he appears to be parodying the device, while at others he uses it with a strength that no one else equalled.

Such a categorization as I have just attempted is not original, it is a commonplace of literary history. Nor is it complete, as a description of the styles available to Elizabethans. And in one way it is confusing for the modern reader, for we tend, nowadays, to think of literary 'schools' as mutually exclusive: we know, for example, that William Carlos Williams wrote much of his best poetry during the last fifteen years of Thomas Hardy's life, but he never wrote like Hardy, nor did Hardy ever write like Williams. John Hollander has said, 'For a true poet, we feel today, all occasions, subjects, forms and conventions must come under the absolute command of one governing style', and he goes on to point out that no such feeling obtained with the Elizabethans.[1] The earlier plain style continued to be available, and some of the best poetry of Sidney, Shakespeare, Jonson, and Donne is written in it. Thomas Churchyard, one of the most plodding poets of the plain style, was made welcome at Wilton, from which the 'New Poetry' had emerged. He was evidently considered a senior poet worthy of respect whose style had not been rejected. And we find many poets between 1575 and 1600 who wrote in the plain style and in the Petrarchan and even in the metaphysical as well. Ralegh is one who can be taken as a kind of epitome of Elizabethan poetry, moving through the different styles and never relinquishing what he learned from each. Another is Greville.

III   Caelica: Early Poems

If the poems in Caelica are in chronological order, as is likely, then

---

[1] John Hollander, Introduction, Ben Jonson (Laurel Poetry Series), 1961, p. 13.

we notice that at certain times the dominant Elizabethan styles coexist in Greville's work, though he starts by being most interested in the Petrarchan experiment, and though in the later poems he deliberately changes to a plain style. Of course, there is variety not only in what he is attempting but in the success of the attempts: of the 109 poems in the collection there are several outright failures, several stiff pieces of writing similar to the dullest parts of the *Treatises*, and several formulary sonnets that never get beyond their formulae. But we re-read a poet for his best poems, and with Greville as with many other poets it is interesting to read his failures, since they help us better to understand his successes.

In the earliest of the love poems alone, we are already confronted by an extraordinary richness and diversity. Some of them recall to me poems, probably written later, by other poets. To speak of these resemblances is not to display my own perspicuity, nor is it to suggest that others looted Greville's manuscripts. It is to suggest the persistence of certain traditions. Nowadays the journalistic critical cliché about a young poet is to say that 'he has found his own voice', the emphasis being on his differentness, on the uniqueness of his voice, on the fact that he sounds like nobody else. But the Elizabethans at their best as well as at their worst are always sounding like each other. They did not search much after uniqueness of voice: what Gascoigne was perfecting, what Sidney was exploring, were usable styles in which the individual could have the freedom to do the most he was capable of, styles which could be inherited by and shared with others who had the talent. It would hardly have struck them that a style could be used for display of personality. So it is not surprising that we notice resemblances to more famous poems in this early work of Greville's. There is the eloquence of 'The world, that all contains, is ever moving' (VII), an extended sonnet and one of the best examples of that Elizabethan kind (of which Shakespeare's 'When to the sessions of sweet silent thought' is another) in which the mutability of the world is considered by the poet, and then is abruptly contradicted by the contemplation of the loved one, who has the permanence of a Platonic Form. In a poem like 'Why how now Cupid, do you covet change?' (XX), a sonnet very far from the rather frigid sonnet-exercises that are also present in *Caelica*, ingenuity of thought combines with a conversational directness rather similar to what we sometimes find in Drayton and Donne. And in 'I, with whose

FULKE GREVILLE

colours Myra dress'd her head' (XXII), the pastoral simplesse and mellifluous loveliness of line suggest the better-known but later songs of Lodge and Greene—almost, but not quite, over-pretty.

> I, that on Sunday at the church-stile found
> A garland sweet, with true-love knots in flowers,
> Which I to wear about mine arm was bound,
> That each of us might know that all was ours:
>   Must I now lead an idle life in wishes?
>   And follow Cupid for his loaves, and fishes?

Of the last line, Bullough comments, 'he does not want to be merely one among five thousand, dependent on miracles for his sustenance.'[1] For Cupid is the Christ of the religion of love. And on a closer inspection it is not hard to see how far this pastoral is from a real country song. Rather, it is in that Elizabethan convention in which the already anglicized secular Mariolatry of the troubadours rejoins its later development, Petrarchanism (a double tradition to become so overworked by the 1590s that it would be ribaldly parodied by Shakespeare and Donne). In Greville's early poetry we find the lover as acolyte or worshipper in that religion where Cupid takes the place of Christ and the mistress the place of either Mary or God. She is moreover a cruel mistress—she is desired sexually and she rejects him sexually, and perhaps rejects him outright. To complicate matters, the whole is often conceived in a pastoral setting of great formality, the formality of which we may not recognize at once, since often there are also present echoes of real folk-songs (as in the line 'Fools only hedge the cuckoo in', from LII, 'Away with these self-loving lads'). Such religious-pastoral metaphors were becoming commonplaces, but when Greville and Sidney first used them they were still metaphors with potential, neither meaningless nor meaningful in themselves.

What Greville was able to do within the tradition which he was helping to define is seen very interestingly in X, 'Love, of man's wandering thoughts the restless being', not a pastoral but fully Petrarchan. It is neither so inventive nor so attractive as the poems I have just mentioned, but it is worth while examining closely, since it shows him exploring the methods and metaphors in a clean

[1] *Poems and Dramas*, vol. 1, p. 241 n.

and workmanlike manner : and it is a kind of starting point which is already full of hints of later directions. This is the first stanza :

> Love, of man's wandering thoughts the restless being,
> Thou from my mind with glory wast invited,
> Glory of those fair eyes, where all eyes, seeing
> Virtue's and beauty's riches, are delighted;
> What angel's pride, or what self-disagreeing,
> What dazzling brightness hath your beams benighted,
>> That fallen thus from those joys which you aspired,
>> Down to my darken'd mind you are retired?

Love, we see, is practically an allegorical quality, since it existed before the mistress invited it out of Greville's mind, and the first line suggests that it existed even before it had an object. It becomes like an angel, specifically Lucifer. The mistress is Godlike in her dazzling brightness, and Love falls, back into Greville's mind, which therefore becomes Hell. The writing of the stanza is formal and rhetorical without being grandiloquent; fluent and clean but barely holding itself this side of cliché : the first line and later the word 'self-disagreeing' are so far all there is to reassure us that we have not read this poem before. At the same time, the hyperbolic metaphor is handled with exceptional care : for Greville at this point suggests, he does not yet quite state, that God, Lucifer and Hell are in the poem.

But in the second stanza, the lover's mind bears all the marks of Hell :

> Within which mind since you from thence ascended,
> Truth clouds itself, wit serves but to resemble,
> Envy is king, at others' good offended,
> Memory doth worlds of wretchedness assemble,
> Passion to ruin passion is intended,
> My reason is but power to dissemble;
>> Then tell me Love, what glory you divine
>> Yourself can find within this soul of mine?

Here the formality of demeanour remains constant, but the type of perception emerging from the conceit of the fallen angel shows the peculiar direction Greville was already able to give to the convention. 'Memory doth worlds of wretchedness assemble.' The line has the Elizabethan fullness that we find in certain other lines of

Greville's (the adequacy and beauty of, for example, 'A simple goodness in the flesh refin'd' or, speaking about children, 'They cry to have, and cry to cast away'). The language of the line is general, but it is a different kind of generality from that of the first stanza, where he was picking his way between certain risks of taste: the generality here is a summation of experience and not an evasion of it. 'Assemble', seeming in the first instant a neutral and innocuous word, in the next is seen as shockingly accurate: this is what memory does do in a period of unhappiness, it deliberately and carefully and painstakingly reconstructs the past causes of present misery, with the perverse result that the accuracy and completeness of its reconstruction only increases the misery. Love, we see, is something so vital that when it is unshared, when it is in exile and has no willingly accepting object, it creates confusion and conflict by its very vitality, and becomes a kind of malignancy. The mind to which Love is exiled is dominated by frustration and deprived of the mistress, like Lucifer in Hell, who is dominated by desires for his past state and deprived of God. But unlike Lucifer, this fallen angel is given a second chance, which is described in the last stanza:

> Rather go back unto that heavenly choir
> Of Nature's riches, in her beauties placed,
> And there in contemplation feed desire,
> Which till it wonder, is not rightly graced;
> For those sweet glories, which you do aspire,
> Must as ideas only be embraced,
>> Since excellence in other form enjoyed,
>> Is by descending to her saints destroyed.

He is allowed to try again, he may return. He must cease desiring her physically but he may embrace her as an idea, or rather as the Idea, the Form of forms, a secular absolute. The last stanza returns us to the manner of the first. We have had a short glimpse of things as we know they are, and we go back now to a theoretical and formulary love, such as can only exist on paper. The Platonic-Petrarchan commonplaces are conveyed with tact and carefulness of language that does not allow the hyperboles to become ridiculous. But the poem is more than an exercise. It succeeds because the commonplaces are darkened, in the middle stanza, with an accuracy of feeling which takes us far beyond the mere conceit, and thus by juxtaposition gives the formulary bits a validity they would not otherwise have.

Deprivation and despair are themes probably no more common in Greville's than in most people's love poems, but he makes them his peculiar province, even as early as this, by the intensity of his apprehension of them. And as we go through *Caelica* we notice more and more how these intensely-apprehended themes are the characteristic of Greville's handling of the love-conventions.

IV   *Caelica: Middle Poems*

A poem like XLV ('Absence, the noble truce') treats of an associated subject, absence, but very differently. The cause of deprivation in 'Love, of man's wandering thoughts the restless being' appeared to be rejection, or conditional rejection, by the mistress; but here the deprivation is caused simply by a geographical separation for a certain time. The tone of much of the poem is witty and sceptical : addressing Absence, Greville says,

> When bankrupt Cupid braveth,
> Thy mines his credit saveth,
> With sweet delays.

The paradox is that absence enables the lover to live up to his protestations by increasing his love, because absence makes the heart grow fonder. But the tone of the careful courtier is preserved at the same time. Lest such lines seem too uncomplimentary, however true they may be, they are balanced by the delicate flattery of :

> Absence, like dainty clouds,
> On glorious bright,
> Nature weak senses shrouds,
> From harming light.

That is, absence shields his eyes from her dazzling light, which he is too weak to contemplate for long. Her light is no longer that of God, but in this poem merely that of the sun. Then the series of conceits praising Absence turns, logically enough, into a derogation of Presence. In the mistress's presence he desires her sexually; but, he goes on, continuing the metaphor of light,

> Absence is free :
> Thoughts do in absence venter
> On Cupid's shadow'd centre,
> They wink and see.

With the naming of 'Cupid's shadow'd centre', referring back not only to the 'dainty clouds' of the earlier image but to the darkness of his lust, the tone itself becomes shadowed by the fact that they are separated, and the desire to swallow incompleteness of experience in the completions of epigrammatic conceits is slackened. Memory doth worlds of wretchedness assemble.

> But thoughts be not so brave,
> With absent joy;
> For you with that you have
> Yourself destroy :
> The absence which you glory,
> Is that which makes you sorry,
> And burn in vain :
> For thought is not the weapon,
> Wherewith thought's ease men cheapen,
> Absence is pain.

Thought of her, after all, is not the means by which he can cheaply obtain 'thought's ease'. Each stanza has ended with a line of two feet, and the poem must end with such a line also. But the last line here is more abruptly separated from the preceding statement than are the last lines in the previous stanzas, and it differs from them also in consisting of a trochee and an iamb rather than of two iambs, so giving the line an additional separating emphasis. It is a slight device, but one which has a considerable effect, for a small change in the context of regular repetition has the effect of a big change in an irregular context. It is set apart, abrupt, even though the statements before it lead up to it logically enough. Absence *is* pain, after all, and the ingenuity of one's conceits is merely a concealment of real feeling.

But the act of concealment is also a proof of there being something to conceal. In the light of the ending, the ingenuity of the conceits can be seen not as mere trifling but as psychologically functional in the poem. One does try to smile things out, to joke about them, until the smiles and jokes begin to cut too deeply into the emotions they are covering. And one of the marks of Greville's love poems is the penetration and accuracy with which they describe the perversity of human emotions. Bullough points out the frequency, throughout Greville's poetry, of compounds prefixed 'self'. In 'Love, of man's wandering thoughts the restless being', it was when love was imprisoned in the underworld of the self that it got infected. And in states of deprivation one is left with merely the elements of the self warring together, for the self is part of fallen Nature, and can only become refined with assistance from outside—from God, that is, or from the lady (who is a God-substitute).

The implications of self-defeat are fully explored in LVI, 'All my senses, like beacons' flame', a poem about sexual action not taken. In theme it is very similar to Sidney's great sonnet 'I might, unhappy word, ah me, I might'. Each is one of the best poems its author wrote, and yet there is a world of contrast in their treatment of their common theme. Sidney uses largely plain speech in his poem, allowing a very dramatic verse movement to do much of the work in conveying the bursts and hesitations of his emotion, while Greville is ornate in his imagery and elaborate in his strategy. In the last poem discussed he had clearly mastered the 'conceited' love-convention, but here he projects it so far from its beginnings that if the poem were anonymous we would swear that it was written in the mid-seventeenth century rather than at the end of the sixteenth.

The poem is in seven-syllable tetrameter lines, a difficult metre that tends to stiffness because of the rather heavy emphasis given to the first syllable of the line. But it is used here with great flexibility; and it is particularly brisk at the start, where the lover himself is brisk, determined to seduce Cynthia. Her name should already give us a clue to the outcome of the poem, for Cynthia is chastity herself and cannot be seduced, but the lover does not realize this. He is a lusty young warrior, confident and vigorous—and rash, as it turns out. He goes to her, and apparently finds her asleep, naked. Under the night sky he is led into a kind of vision of the gods, among whom he finds himself. Yet his is a false confidence. He becomes the child of his fantasy and loses his chance. (It is not at once clear what has happened in the literal situation, but later in line 35 we gather that she has been 'unkind', and finally in lines 45–8 that he has delayed when he could have taken her.)

> I stepp'd forth to touch the sky,
> I a god by Cupid dreams,
> Cynthia who did naked lie,
> Runs away like silver streams;
> Leaving hollow banks behind,
> Who can neither forward move,
> Nor if rivers be unkind,
> Turn away or leave to love.

The imagery thus far in the poem has been continuously linked; but the transition in the fourth line quoted is almost surrealistic, where the moonlight becomes water draining away. For she is pure light— not that of God, or even the sun this time, but the silver light of the moon. He is left standing by the dried river bed, on the banks and also *like* them, for banks normally clasp the stream but here they clasp nothing. 'There stand I' he goes on—and fairly deliberately there is a sexual metaphor implied.

> There stand I, like Arctic Pole,
> Where Sol passeth o'er the line,
> Mourning my benighted soul,
> Which so loseth light divine.

He has lost all light now. Even water is inaccessible, being turned to ice. He stands desperate, isolated, and sterile, like the Pole, which Greville seems to visualize as something actually pole-like, or maybe even as a kind of mountain. Then there is a transition.

> There stand I like men that preach
> From the execution place,
> At their death content to teach
> All the world with their disgrace:

The lonely figure and its background melt surreally, for the last time, into a similar constant figure against another background. Now he is doomed, he is a living example of what not to do or be. The image of the man making his speech from the scaffold leads easily to the concluding lines (which constitute that speech) on a traditional theme fully brought to life by delicate rueful ironies.

He dies because *she* did not 'die'—in the second sense, of sexual orgasm, that the Elizabethans were endlessly fond of giving to the word. The condemned man's advice to lovers is to waste no time in dreaming or in idealizing: for love is 'Nature's art', it is earthly or it is nothing. The poem ends,

> None can well behold with eyes,
> But what underneath him lies.

While he was a god in the heaven of his imagination, the real Cynthia was still on earth. Moreover, the ideal is 'above' man, while sex is 'beneath' him, a lower sort of activity. And Cynthia lying there as he stands by her bed is also physically beneath him. The resemblance to Marvell here becomes uncanny: it was already there in the fantasy and ingenuity of the transformations—each image clear and hard in itself but melting easily, though surprisingly, into the next; it was there in the mixture of lyricism and irony bathing the whole poem; it is here most of all in the complexity of meaning in the last two lines. It is as good a poem as the best of Marvell's, and for something like the reasons that Marvell is good: it is the result of a confrontation between, on the one hand, an awareness of the grace and delicacy of courtly love at its best, and, on the other, an equally full awareness of the way things are in life itself, where such idealism is simply irrelevant.

I have so far disregarded those numerous poems in which Greville uses a style largely free of imagery. They are an important part, even of his early work, but they are not the whole of Greville. His earlier intention seems to have been to explore the ornate conventions to their utmost, and he certainly carried them to their extreme in the metaphysical imagery of LXVIII ('While that my heart an altar I did make') and of LXI ('Caelica, while you do swear that you do love me best'). (The latter at one point even topples into the slightly ludicrous effects that such imagery always risks:

> The leaves fall off, when sap goes to the root,
> The warmth doth clothe the bough again;
> And to the dead tree what doth boot,
> The silly man's manuring pain?)

It is not true that Greville seems ill at ease in the ornate poems, as has sometimes been implied. He mastered the Petrarchan convention, and experimented widely and successfully in a number of styles, from the 'artless' pastoralism of 'I, with whose colours Myra dress'd her head' or 'Away with these self-loving lads' to the high sophistication and rather troubled elaboration of the poem just discussed. In these poems alone he stands with the best of the Elizabethans and early Jacobeans, because his ingenuity seldom escapes from the facts of the world: absence, after all, is pain; love is only Nature's art—and his regret at such facts is expressed cleanly, artfully, and movingly.

V Nature and the Need for Authority

After the love poems there is a short miscellaneous group, which is followed by a pair of sonnets, LXXXIV ('Farewell sweet boy, complain not of my truth') and LXXXV ('Love is the peace, whereto all thoughts do strive'), the one a farewell to love, and the other a definition of Christian love which also serves as introduction to the final group of poems. The farewell to love is something of a convention in Elizabethan sonnet sequences, and though *Caelica* is not actually such a sequence it had probably been intended as one at some time or other. But to say it is a convention explains nothing: everything depends on why an author picks a particular convention and on what he does with it. I want to show how this farewell to love and the poem following it are inevitable for Greville given the maturing of his attitudes. Earthly love had to be rejected, sooner or later, because the older one becomes the more clearly one sees through the Platonic rubbish of a poem like 'Love, of man's wandering thoughts the restless being'; and if one sees through that then one is left with a love that is 'only Nature's art', a relationship with another human being which even if lasting and meaningful must take place within Nature, and must be subject to her laws. And Nature, for a Christian of the Renaissance, is flawed.

There is much that is difficult to grasp about Greville's views, particularly those he holds about Nature. Perhaps, as G. A. Wilkes has suggested, we find his attitudes so self-contradictory because we are ignorant of the exact chronology of the writings.[1] This may be so, but we are still left with the apparently deliberate juxta-

---

[1] G. A. Wilkes, 'The Sequence of Writings of Fulke Greville, Lord Brooke', *Studies in Philology* LVI, 3, pp. 489–503.

position of the two final choruses of *Mustapha*. U. M. Ellis Fermor says of them :

> In the first chorus he takes the Lucretian 'Nature' as the symbol of a beneficent controlling power, but in the second, he reverses Lucretius's conclusion, sees Nature herself as the source of evil and comes, simultaneously, very near to equating this 'Nature' with God. . . . He first condemns superstition and commits man to natural law and then, in a further reach of destructive thought, condemns that natural law itself.[1]

In *Caelica*, though he has not yet brought his thought to such extreme opposed positions, he already sees Nature as by turns attractive and repulsive. Nevertheless, it does seem possible to sort out his attitudes on the subject as they appear in *Caelica*, even if the sorting out may result in something of an over-simplification. Nature is attractive, and moreover we are born into it, but there are two things wrong with it : first, it is a rival to God in attracting our worship; secondly, it is fallen, along with man, and so is mutable.

It is a rival to God, although created by him, in that man may love the particulars of Nature as an end in themselves. In XCVI ('In those years, when our sense, desire and wit') 'the wealth of Nature' is seen as a temptation and an obstacle. Nature is the 'fair usurper',

> Yet rules she none, but such as will obey,
> And to that end becomes what they aspire.

And in CII ('The serpent, Sin, by showing human lust') he even considers what would happen if there were no God :

> But grant that there were no eternity,
> That life were all, and pleasure life of it,
> In sin's excess there yet confusions be,
> Which spoil his peace, and passionate his wit,
>   Making his nature less, his reason thrall,
>   To tyranny of vice unnatural.
>
> And as hell-fires, not wanting heat, want light;
> So these strange witchcrafts, which like pleasure be,
> Not wanting fair enticements, want delight,

[1] U. M. Ellis Fermor, Introduction, *Caelica*.

Inward being nothing but deformity;
But do at open doors let frail powers in
To that strait building, Little-ease of sin.

For, as part of fallen Nature, we contain our own confusions. The possibility of a hell in the human mind anticipating the Hell after death is a constant theme of Greville's. Another theme, an almost universal preoccupation of medieval and Elizabethan writers, is that of the mutability of all Nature. Nature is not only fallen, she is finite, subject to time and thus to change. In the third chorus of *Mustapha*, both Time and Eternity say, accurately, 'I am the measure of felicity.' But the two felicities are of a different sort. For Time's 'essence only is to write, and blot'. If you put your trust in the temporal and the finite, you are putting your trust in what will inevitably fail you.

The last observation was not new, nor was it confined to Elizabethans. Similarly Camus called life in a temporal world without sanction 'absurd', but Camus did not discover this fact : he merely put more abruptly what many men have noticed. Interestingly enough, Camus also used the image of Little-ease (*le malconfort*), the cell where one cannot stand, sit, or lie, for the state of a man constrained by a sense of guilt in a world where there is no god and thus where there can be no redemption for that guilt.

> Il fallait vivre dans le malconfort. . . . Tous les jours, par l'immuable contrainte qui ankylosait son corps, le condamné apprenait qu'il était coupable et que l'innocence consiste à s'étirer joyeusement.[1]

What is important is not so much the perception of absurdity, which to a certain kind of thinker is inevitable,[2] as how one conducts oneself after making that perception. Camus's great contribution is less in the analysis of the sickness into which we are born than in the determination to live with that sickness, fully acknowledging it and accepting it as the basis for our actions. Greville could not make such an acceptance.

He was supersensitive to the dangers of attempting to stand on

---

[1] Albert Camus, *La Chute*, Paris 1956, pp. 126–7.
[2] To a certain kind of thinker in the West, that is. But there have also been those, from the Cathars to the pantheists and the modern heirs of the pantheists, who have viewed the world as a place where paradise can be re-created by the rejection of all intellectual process.

one's own. Thus the crying need for authority, which, by the time of *Humane Learning*, can lead him into the peculiarly repellent position of advocating terror as a political expedient in the unified authoritarian state.[1] Those who have a constant sense of human depravity end up by being able to trust only in the abstraction of authoritarianism. And Greville, though he varies in his attitude to political authoritarianism (aware as he is of the fallibility of princes), is constant in putting ultimate trust only in the Divine ideal.

It would be a mistake to say that Greville's set of attitudes were forced on him by his time alone. There were other schools of thought available—there was, for example, a strong movement by the end of the sixteenth century for an almost complete religious toleration; but Greville was more interested in Calvin's thought with its emphasis on unity and authority. On earth he could be certain only of the weakness, mutability, and uncertainty of all that surrounded him; and this conviction is very clear in some of the religious poems where he tries to surrender himself to God, and succeeds in that surrender only with a desperation of voice very similar to that of Donne in the Divine Poems.

How one should live the temporal life, ultimately, is by hardly living at all. Those who will reach Heaven, the elect, are described thus in the prologue to *Alaham*:

> Those angel-souls in flesh imprisoned,
> · Like strangers living in mortality,
> Still more, and more, themselves enspirited,
> Refining Nature to eternity;
> By being maids in earth's adulterous bed.

The rigour of such a belief gives additional force to such lines as 'The flesh is dead, before grace can be born' (LXXXIX), or 'For God comes not, till man be overthrown;/Peace is the seed of grace, in dead flesh sown' (XCVI). They may be Pauline commonplaces, but they are intended very literally and very passionately by Greville.

---

[1] Greville, *Treatise of Humane Learning*, stanza 92. He is speaking of secular laws:
> Therefore, as shadows of those laws divine,
> They must assist Church-censure, punish error,
> Since when, from order, nature would decline,
> There is no other native cure but terror;
> By discipline, to keep the doctrine free,
> That Faith and Power still relatives may be.

Practically any value in life is denied except as a preparation for death.

The rejection of life's secular particulars changes not only the subject matter of *Caelica* but the style. Such particulars are evil because they divert man from the abstraction toward which he should be labouring to elevate himself; earth is an adulterous bed, and thus in abandoning the ornate style, which is loaded with the lushness of the finite, Greville is rejecting its inducements stylistically as well.

It is not only a rejection, of course, it is also an acceptance.

> Love is the peace, whereto all thoughts do strive,
> Done and begun with all our power in one:
> The first and last in us that is alive,
> End of the good, and therewith pleas'd alone.
>
> Perfection's spirit, goddess of the mind,
> Passed through hope, desire, grief and fear,
> A simple goodness in the flesh refin'd,
> Which of the joys to come doth witness bear.
>
> Constant, because it sees no cause to vary,
> A quintessence of passions overthrown,
> Rais'd above all that change of objects carry,
> A nature by no other nature known:
>   For glory's of eternity a frame,
>   That by all bodies else obscures her name.

Our love for God is both a way to the absolute, and—being an image or imitation of God's love—is in another sense already of the absolute, the end itself. The poem is a beautiful piece of Protestant literature; and the line 'A simple goodness in the flesh refin'd' is a beautiful expression of the Protestant ideal. 'Refine' is one of Greville's favourite words, and it is surely an important word for an understanding of the relation between the particulars of the life the Christian leads and the absolute beyond it. But it is also a useful word to describe what Greville is now attempting to do with his style: for the language itself is being 'refined' of the heavy impurities of the life of this world. The poem, almost void of imagery, gentle and firm in tone, complex in thought but lucid in syntax and language (one cannot always say this of Greville), is one of the triumphs of the plain style, and introduces a section of Greville's poems full of such triumphs.

VI   *Caelica: Late Poems*

The preceding outline ends as a description of attitudes that I find at best sterile and at worst obnoxious. Of course one has to have a historical sense when discussing ideas of the past. Certain needs at a certain time in history, certain insensitivities which may have counterparts in different but equally extreme modern insensitivities, may account for and on occasion excuse ideas of the past which one finds repugnant. But a poem must be more than the ideas it contains. If it cannot validate itself without one's having to make historical allowances, then it is not likely to be very good. And the poem just quoted does validate the ideas that I had summarized. It puts them in terms of the imagination and makes humane what I would have otherwise called inhumane attitudes; it makes the higher good convincing; and in it love is not the necessity of siding with an authoritarian God but an attempt to capture, and be part of, the rhythm of a divinely created universe.

In many of the following poems a similar validation occurs. In them Greville has moved, as Donne was to do a little later, from the paradoxes of love to the paradoxes of Christianity. The move was an obvious one, given their decision to put away what they considered childish things. The metaphors of worship used in courtly love were originally a translation from the terms of Christian worship, and so now it was a matter of translating them back. Deprivation of the unkind or absent mistress becomes deprivation of God's grace. The mistress had been an absolute, an ideal, an unchangeable, as contrasted to the flawed, fallen, and changeable particulars of creation : so is God.

Most of these poems are written more straightforwardly than those earlier in *Caelica*, and their tone is more consistently serious. God is not to be trifled with, or subjected to ambiguities. The craving for certainty of grace is painful. The *intermittences du cœur* which had provoked, before, a witty shrug, a rueful attempt to joke it out, a depression of the spirits, become now the cause for un-qualified lamentation. The change was deliberate and conscious. Greville says in the *Life of Sidney* :

For my own part, I found my creeping genius more fixed upon the images of life, than the images of wit, and therefore chose not to write to them on whose foot the black ox had not already trod, as the proverb is, but to those only, that are weatherbeaten in the sea of this world, such as having lost the sight of their gardens and groves, study to sail on a right course among rocks and quicksands.

When he speaks about 'images of life', Greville is not suggesting the adoption of some kind of sixteenth-century Imagism, he means something like 'reality'. And for him reality had increasingly become a religious matter.

One of the most impressive of these poems is C, on night, which at first sight seems a little out of place among the religious poems. It could be read as a description, simply, of certain common psychological weaknesses. But to do so would be to only partially read it.

> In night when colours all to black are cast,
> Distinction lost, or gone down with the light;
> The eye a watch to inward senses plac'd,
> Not seeing, yet still having power of sight,
>
> Gives vain alarums to the inward sense,
> Where fear stirr'd up with witty tyranny,
> Confounds all powers, and thorough self-offence,
> Doth forge and raise impossibility :
>
> Such as in thick depriving darknesses,
> Proper reflections of the error be,
> And images of self-confusednesses,
> Which hurt imaginations only see;
>   And from this nothing seen, tells news of devils,
>   Which but expressions be of inward evils.

The first four lines consist of a careful, concise, and accurate description of nightfall and its effect on a man. The observing intelligence is already making itself felt, even in the internal commas of the second and fourth lines, making careful distinctions even about that state in which distinction is lost. It emerges more openly in the second quatrain, in which it both describes and explains.

'Witty tyranny' is the tyranny of wit, or the mind, *on its own*, without outside assistance. One's delusions in darkness, one's 'self-offence', similarly, are the result of a simple dependence on the self rather than on the external, which could act as check and guide : in daylight one can at least depend on external fact (Nature) in order to keep one's sense of proportion. In the ninth line, the state of mind is compared explicitly with the 'thick depriving darknesses' of Hell, where the images (devils, perhaps) are moral error's own reflections. For Elizabethan mirrors reflect in an exemplary fashion, and show here the essence of what is. Superficially it seems a thoroughly rationalistic poem explaining delusion in an almost Freudian way as the result of 'hurt imagination' and 'inward evils', as repression emerging in dream or hallucination, but the whole emphasis of the poem (one should not even need the context of *Caelica*) is on the real Hell, of which the night is simply image, and on the authority, that of God, of which one is deprived.

The previous poem, 'Down in the depth of mine iniquity', treats of the deprivation of God more directly. In this part of *Caelica* Greville is much preoccupied with the genuineness of prayer. Too often we pray

> Thinking a wish may wear out vanity,
> Or habits be by miracles defac'd.

This poem is not a prayer but a meditation; nevertheless the feeling behind it is similar to that of a man praying : it is governed by the same moral bracing, by the effort to see things as they really are, by the Protestant concern with sincerity. Most of the lines end with the double rhymes Greville is so fond of, and here they help to convey the difficulty, the lack of ease, the strain it imposes on a man to meditate honestly on such a subject and to work his way through to its conclusion.

> Down in the depth of mine iniquity,
> That ugly centre of infernal spirits;
> Where each sin feels her own deformity,
> In those peculiar torments she inherits,
>   Depriv'd of human graces, and divine,
>   Even there appears this saving God of mine.

For comparison and contrast we can think back to the tenth poem : it is almost as though the most important part of Greville's poetry

consisted of an attempt to chart the map of Hell. The later poem
starts with a description of the state of sin, all the more terrifying
for the lack of melodramatic demons: for the Hell here, like that
of the poem on night, is caused by deprivation alone. The sinner is
in Little-ease, unable to achieve the simple relief of stretching his
limbs. Deprivation causes the self to become malignant, and to
inherit that torment to which divine grace is an immunization, the
torment in which sin recognizes its deformity and can do nothing
to change it. The refrain, however, contains a surprise, and flatly
juxtaposes the 'saving God'. Nothing in the stanza has prepared us
for this: the apprehension of God's grace, at this point of the poem,
is something totally illogical, blind faith.

> And in this fatal mirror of transgression,
> Shows man as fruit of his degeneration,
> The error's ugly infinite impression,[1]
> Which bears the faithless down to desperation;
> > Depriv'd of human graces and divine,
> > Even there appears this saving God of mine.

The mirror is again exemplary, but the example here is of God
himself (who is in CIX, also, the 'mirror of transgression'). The
error, reflected in God, shows up in all its implications: man is
degenerate, and fallen, and there is little he can do about it. The
vowel-alliteration of the third line makes it easy to say quickly; the
error's 'impression' spreads, similarly, with the ease and speed of a
stain on water. The despair is absolute. But again, so is God, and
the second refrain has a similar effect to the first, God as saviour
re-entering the poem as flat affirmation.

> In power and truth, almighty and eternal,
> Which on the sin reflects strange desolation,
> With glory scourging all the sprites infernal,
> And uncreated hell with unprivation;
> > Depriv'd of human graces, not divine,
> > Even there appears this saving God of mine.

What the presence of God can do is here described: he negates the
negative, and he applies to Hell, the state of privation, its opposite

---

[1] As Yvor Winters has pointed out, this line is the subject of the verb
'shows'.

—'unprivation'. And now the refrain can change, for the soul is thus not deprived of divine grace. But we still do not know *how* God has brought his grace to bear on the individual soul.

> For on this spiritual cross condemned lying,
> To pains infernal by eternal doom,
> I see my Saviour for the same sins dying,
> And from that hell I fear'd, to free me, come;
>   Depriv'd of human graces, not divine,
>   Thus hath his death rais'd up this soul of mine.

The rigour of his contemplation has now enabled the speaker to visualize Christ and has given him understanding of his grace. The contemplation is difficult: the first line of the stanza, heavy with consonants, gives a sense of difficulty barely overcome, but it is overcome—and in the fourth line the very punctuation, helping to define the movement, indicates firmness and confidence. In the refrain, the soul is still deprived of human grace, but it is triumphant partaker of divine grace, and the word 'Thus' at the start of the last line makes the appearance of God no longer the illogicality it was in the first stanza but something logical and inevitable. God saves by pains that are greater than those that were experienced by man in the first stanza, and the mirror becomes an instrument no longer of chastisement but of forgiveness and divine compassion. This is one of the great religious poems because the grave, strong, agonized mind is exercised to the full, working *with* the feeling throughout the meditation. The feeling is tense and clenched and never self-indulgent: faith provides it with hope, but it calls on the mind to explain how that hope can be fulfilled. And the needed assurance of God's saving power does not remain merely the illogical assertion of faith: it is embodied in the entire complex experience of the poem.

The last poem in *Caelica*, 'Sion lies waste', bears certain resemblances to it; both are written in the same stanza-pattern, with the insistent refrain that finally changes and the sonority of the Latinate double rhymes, and both share the theme of man's degeneration. But here we do not have a description of Hell in an individual soul; instead the poem speaks about the corruption of social man.

> Sion lies waste, and thy Jerusalem,
> O Lord, is fall'n to utter desolation,

Against thy prophets, and thy holy men,
The sin hath wrought a fatal combination,
   Profan'd thy name, thy worship overthrown,
   And made thee living Lord, a God unknown.

In this poem the simplicity of language, the directness of tone, and the lively variations in the verse movement, all serve to insist on the personal grief behind the public utterance. It is still a grief, however, that can sharply analyse : Greville never allows his feeling to eliminate his mind. God is a 'living Lord', a 'living light', but man's degeneration has its own life too, like the chemical changes in a rotting apple, and the multiplicity of that life must be itemized and described so that it may be recognized and rejected.

And rejected for what?

   That sensual unsatiable vast womb
   Of thy seen Church, thy unseen Church disgraceth.

The unseen Church is the abstraction, the ideal, the Form of what the seen Church should be. Again we see the Platonism which dominated Greville, and has dominated Christianity; and later we have God once more as exemplary mirror, his image being a 'sinless pure impression'. An abstraction cannot change, yet paradoxically God is an abstraction that is living, and he is not subject on the one hand to the state of inertia implied by the purely theoretical abstractions or on the other to the state of flux implied by the temporally living.

But in this poem God is a hope, rather than the present fact that he was in 'Down in the depth'. Greville ends imploring 'sweet Jesus, fill up time, and come', but the tone does not have the assurance of the end of the earlier poem : there is still desperation behind the grief, desperation in the attitude that must reject all of life and find in it only corruption, interpreting absurdity as wickedness, seeing the only way to live as 'maids in earth's adulterous bed', and holding out for an abstraction of complete purity which can never be possessed on earth.

The idea that life is vanity was held by most intelligent men of the Renaissance. Yet many of them evidently did not reinforce their thought with their feelings : life is vanity, perhaps, but meanwhile they could turn to an enjoyment of the world, for which they could always repent on the deathbed. Greville is different, I think, because his thought is reinforced by a propensity to despair. He was too strict, too honest with himself, too consistent, to disregard what both his mind and his emotions told him. In the last poems of *Caelica*, much of the greatness lies in the clarity and strength of the poignancy he gives to the despair that can be cured only by the end of life. And in these poems, too, the body cries out in pain at the rejections it is being forced to make, and in the note of the cry we recognize the very humanity it is a cry against.

HARDY AND THE BALLADS

I

John Crowe Ransom has called Hardy a Victorian poet, and it is certainly true that Hardy wrote quite a lot of his poetry during the Victorian era. Even though his first book of it was not published until 1898, many of the poems in later volumes are followed by nineteenth-century dates. And the characteristics of Hardy's poetic style, for better or worse, are fully defined in all he wrote before 1900. It improves, but it does not become different in kind. On the other hand we often find Hardy treated like Hopkins as one of the first of the moderns: he and Hopkins, in fact, are the poets we usually find at the start of an anthology of twentieth-century English poetry. And unlike Hopkins he lived well into the twentieth century, for if he was born eight years after the death of Sir Walter Scott, we may notice that toward the end of his life he was reading Proust, whom he both influenced and outlived. So we can find good reason for thinking of Hardy as either a nineteenth-century poet or a twentieth-century poet.

Yet most of the time his poetry is of either century only in rather superficial ways. It is true that there is a lot of Victorian subject-matter and that he produces a lot of Victorian ideas: the social scene is often one that we recognize from novels of the time, and there is much made of evolution, loss of faith, and the death of God. But in his most successful poems (and it is by these that we must define him) the social background is not usually very important, and the ideas are present only in such a general way that they do not belong to specifically Victorian thought. Rather, what we may find in his best poetry is an emotional reaction to ideas, which can be a very different matter.

It is also true that when we come to a poem like 'The Convergence of the Twain', we can find writing like this, in which he describes the shipwrecked *Titanic* at the bottom of the sea :

> Over the mirrors meant
> To glass the opulent
> The sea-worm crawls—grotesque, slimed, dumb, indifferent.

The image may remind us, a touch, of Tennyson or Beddoes. But they would have used it in connection with psychological breakdown, whereas Hardy uses it to show how those most powerful in society are in the end completely powerless before the processes of nature and time. It is a theme as characteristic of other centuries as of the nineteenth—we may think of the fall of magistrates, or of the sea's defeat of Sir Patrick Spens. The statement and the feeling (to put it in another way) do not really belong to any specific time because they are commonplaces of every time. But—we may point out—there is an abruptness, almost a brokenness to the tone, a savagery to the language, that we like to think of as typical of much twentieth-century poetry. Again, though, if we look at the passage closely and in context, we see that it is acting in concert with explicit general statements, in a completely traditional and unfragmentary way, very far from the ways of that generation of modernists with which Hardy's life-span overlapped.

Perhaps my thought might be clearer if I were to take a complete poem. Around the middle of Hardy's collected poetry comes a poem called 'In Time of "The Breaking of Nations" ', and it is about the start of the First World War. It has been often anthologized, but it is easy to underrate because of the simplicity of its expression, and of what may strike the reader as an obviousness to the sentiment.

> Only a man harrowing clods
>   In a slow silent walk
> With an old horse that stumbles and nods
>   Half asleep as they stalk.
>
> Only thin smoke without flame
>   From the heaps of couch grass;

Yet this will go onward the same
   Though Dynasties pass.

Yonder a maid and her wight
   Come whispering by :
War's annals will cloud into night
   Ere their story die.

I wouldn't find the style of this poem very easy to date if I were
to come across it printed anonymously. It is direct and economical,
without drawing attention to itself, though the eye hesitates on
what seem at first a couple of weaknesses in the diction. But as
often in Hardy what at first may seem weak turns out in the end
to be a strength. One of the words is 'stalk'—surely, we think, it
entered the poem only for the rhyme, but then we realize, with our
attention fully upon it, that the word does properly indicate the
stiff, ungraceful movement of the man and the old horse over the
bare earth and, by implication, over the centuries. The phrase 'a
maid and her wight' may jar us too, though only slightly : why
these archaisms, we ask, when a phrase like 'a girl and a boy' would
do as well? But of course the slight archaisms take us out of the
specific year when the poem was written, and help to suggest those
patterns of human and vegetable behaviour that the poem is about.

For between these two images—the one of resigned human labour
to keep the land fruitful and the other of human love which will
end by making the body fruitful—there is the even more powerful
and much more ambiguous one, of couch grass, the perennial weed,
that invades the fields humans have cultivated, and will always
continue to do so, and that has been gathered in heaps to burn by
the humans, who continue their temporary defeats of it. Humans
survive, and *it* survives, in spite of the burning, survives through
its very neutrality, like the 'slimed sea-worm'. It burns in 'thin
smoke without flame'—that is, not violently but continuously. The
image is brief, but sharp, and the struggle between man and the
simplest forms of life is like a parody of all wars. Or, better, we
could say that all wars are like a parody of it, it being the more
elementary struggle.

All flesh is grass : we war against the couch grass as we war
against each other : yet the wars will never completely succeed,
and various human activities will always continue. Put like this,

the poem would amount to no more than truism, but it is saved from such by the succinct clarity of the images of the harrower and the burning weed. The general assertions belong equally to the nineteenth and to the early twentieth century, but in essentials the poem belongs specifically to neither. And the same can be said of pretty well all of Hardy's best poetry.

John Crowe Ransom has said:

> Either he was not influenced by the current styles of poetry that were admired in his lifetime, or else he was not adaptive and could not change from the style which he came into at the outset, as into a style that suited him. For the one reason or the other, he continued in it, though he widened its range.[1]

He continued in it. That is, he didn't go through the dramatic developments of style that we find in many of the writers who have been of most weight for modern readers. James and Yeats have their early, middle, and late styles, but Hardy found quite early a way of writing large and open enough to last him for a long lifetime, and in which he could realize most of his greatest poems.

The reason he is of neither century is the obvious one. The single important influence on him is that of the Ballads, and the majority of his poems derive either directly or indirectly from them. Donald Davidson, writing of the novels, said that

> The characteristic Hardy novel is conceived as a *told* (or *sung*) story, or at least not as a literary story . . . it is an extension, in the form of a modern prose fiction, of a traditional ballad or an oral tale.[2]

If this is so of his prose, how much more obviously it is of his poetry. From beginning to end of his collected poems we find ballads of all varieties, from the laborious 'The Dance at the Phoenix' through the fine melodrama of 'A Trampwoman's Tragedy' to the grotesque dialogue of 'Her Second Husband Hears the Story' in his last book, where a woman in bed with her second husband tells him how she prevented her drunken first husband from making love to her, by sewing him into the sheets of the bed and thus inadver-

[1] J. C. Ransom, 'Honey and Gall', *Southern Review* VI, 1, p. 12.
[2] Donald Davidson, 'The Traditional Basis of Thomas Hardy's Fiction', *Hardy*, ed. Albert J. Guerard (Twentieth Century Views series), Englewood Cliffs N.J., 1963, p. 15.

tently smothering him to death. (As the second husband remarks in the last line, 'Well, it's a cool queer tale!'.)

The ballad so dominates his poetry that when we come to such poems as 'I need not go' or 'I say I'll seek her', we know at once, before we perceive the more direct hints at identity, that the girl in each of the poems is a *dead* sweetheart, because the writing is such that we are given ballad expectations, and we sense that—as in 'The Unquiet Grave'—the living man is still in love with the dead girl. We have a similar kind of expectation when we start reading 'Who's in the Next Room?'.

> 'Who's in the next room?—who?
> I seemed to see
> Somebody in the dawning passing through,
> Unknown to me.'
> 'Nay: you saw naught. He passed invisibly.'
>
> 'Who's in the next room?—who?
> I seem to hear
> Somebody muttering firm in a language new
> That chills the ear.'
> 'No: you catch not his tongue who has entered there.'
>
> 'Who's in the next room?—who?
> I seem to feel
> His breath like a clammy draught, as if it drew
> From the Polar Wheel.'
> 'No: none who breathes at all does the door conceal.'
>
> 'Who's in the next room?—who?
> A figure wan
> With a message to one in there of something due?
> Shall I know him anon?'
> 'Yea he; and he brought such; and you'll know him anon.'

I don't remember my first reading of this poem. But I am pretty certain that I recognized its pattern by the time I reached the end of the first stanza. Who 'passed invisibly' but Death? This is what I mean by ballad expectations. I am not even sure, explicitly, where these expectations come from, being unable to find a precise parallel in any ballad I can remember. The unnamed visitor could of course be a god or an angel, but there are reasons already to be found in that first stanza for our thinking it something less exalted, something fearful yet commonplace, more suited to the tone of the ballad. For we have to remember that gods and angels make virtually no appearance in the Ballads.

Why then, if we were to come to the poem fresh, without even knowing it was by Hardy, do we think of ballads, given the facts that it is not a narrative and that it is not in any kind of ballad-metre? First, I would say, because there is a suggestion of the homely riddle—the riddle being, in the first stanza, 'what is a presence but invisible?', and in the last, 'who collects dues yet is not a tangible person?'. Such riddles belong to all folk-lore, but particularly occur in ballads. Secondly, the poem consists of a dialogue—the first four lines of each stanza spoken by one person, the last lines being the ambiguous answers of the other. The speakers are distinct—the first voice is close to panic, its tone is urgent and suspicious, the second is more measured, and on the whole rather laconic. They are distinct, but we do not know the sex, age, or situation of the first speaker, and of the second we cannot even be sure that it is a mortal: still less is there any suggestion of personality in either. (In the ballad of 'Edward', similarly, there is no suggestion of personality in the voice of either mother or son.) Lastly we think of ballads because of the complete simplicity of language—a simplicity both cause and effect of the author's impersonality: for though he is in fact artful and sophisticated, all the artfulness and sophistication are concealed within the form of the ballad dialogue.

If we can get all this from the first stanza, what does the rest of the poem add? The whole point of the form is that the speaker should ask three questions and get the answer No and that in the final stanza the question should be answered Yes. The poem depends on the pattern of the build, the increasing horror of understanding, all the more because we are familiar with the pattern from ballads and fairy-tales. I have suggested that the poem seems more simple than it really is. The plainness of the language is so tense and controlled that a word that is only slightly unusual can have a disproportionately chilling effect—e.g. the word 'firm' in the phrase 'Somebody muttering firm' already 'chills the ear', even before we are told that it does. There is the brilliant impetuous clumsiness to the first line of each stanza, and by contrast the measured tone of each last line, the poem ending with an almost contemptuous (and almost epigrammatic) dismissal of the questioner: 'Yea he; and he brought such; and you'll see him anon.' There is nothing you can do about it, human being, with all your panic and nerves and longing for explanations.

The poem suggests, without melodrama, all the terrors and strangeness implied by the folk personification of death. Homely and familiar materials, expressed in simple language, are used to produce primitive and rather complex emotions. The poem could not have been written without the old ballads on which it is consciously modelled.

II

Much of Hardy's poetry, then, is literally in ballad-form—that is, it consists of narratives written in the ballad-stanza and ballad-metre. But even in those that are not literally ballads, some or all of the ballad-characteristics are likely to be present. The diction tends to be plain and colloquial, the grotesque and the supernatural are present as a matter of course, and above all the structure of the narrative is economical, with incident and explanation implied wherever possible.

The original Ballads are famous for their economy—for their omissions, their jumps over unnecessary parts of the narrative, and their implications of unstated motive. The most obvious type of omission takes place in the short version of 'Sir Patrick Spens'. Sir Patrick receives the king's message on the sea-shore, and he and his man exchange misgivings about putting to sea at this time of year. The stanza that follows is this:

> O our Scots nobles wer right laith
> To weet their cork-heild schoone:
> Bot lang owre a' the play were playd,
> Thair hats they swam aboone.

Not only are we ignorant of the king's object in sending Sir Patrick on this voyage, not only are we unaware that the voyage has been started, we have gone direct from Sir Patrick's misgivings to the actual sinking of the ship. And the sinking is told us *by implication*, in terms of objects—the cork-heeled shoes and the hats are seen in the sea: thus, we may gather, the nobles themselves are in the sea, and thus the ship they were in must have sunk. That such an economy of narrative did not originate as a conscious literary device can be seen by comparing this version with the longer, equally authentic, and (presumably) earlier version, in which we learn in detail about the objects of the voyage and the sinking of the ship before we reach the stanza I have just quoted. The omissions result, obviously, from the oral tradition: a paring-down took place because singers would remember only what was important, dramatic, and absolutely necessary to the narrative. But the paring-down having taken place, partly through chance, partly through art, partly through forgetfulness, the result is a stylistic device that is one of the most impressive elements of the ballad. The shorter version of 'Sir Patrck Spens', we all agree, is more shapely, more dramatic, cleaner in form, and clearer in direction.

Another and more sophisticated type of omission takes place in the equally famous ballad, 'Edward'. The ballad consists wholly of dialogue, by which action is concealed, questioned, and finally disclosed. The mother asks her son why his sword is bloody. He tells her that the blood is his hawk's, then he says it is his horse's, and finally he admits that he has killed his father. She then asks what penance he will do, what he will do with his possessions and his wife and children, and what he will leave to her, his mother. He answers these questions in turn, and in answer to the last says:

'The curse of hell frae me sall ye beir,
Sic counseils ye gave to me O.'

Here the ballad ends. It is the first hint that we have had that the mother is other than a completely innocent questioner. The revelation that she was less than that turns the poem into something close to catechism, to ritual, to the riddling series of questions asked in dark woods by evil ones who suddenly appear in the traveller's path. The pattern of the poem as it stands is so tight, it so defines the content and justifies the delaying of the information in the last two lines, that it would be hard to expect a longer version to be anything but inferior. The wicked mother's motives need no explanation. The very largeness of possibilities provides a mystery—but all the possibilities are appropriate, and mystery itself is an essential part of the ballad's subject.

So these are two types of omission commonly found in the ballad—omission of narrative incident, and omission of motive and character. We get a paring-down to essentials, and the greater the paring the wider and richer the implications.

A third type of omission occurs in the Aberdeenshire ballad of 'The Laily Worm and the Machrel of the Sea'. This is about a wicked stepmother who transforms her stepson into a serpent and her stepdaughter into a mackerel. The father, perhaps by chance, comes across the serpent, learns the truth, and orders his wife to change them back. She brings the son back to his former shape, but the mackerel-daughter is too proud, and says:

> 'Ye shaped me ance an unseemly shape
> And ye's never more shape me.'

The father then has his wife burned at the stake.

No doubt there have been parings-down in the transmission of this ballad, since such is what we can expect through an oral tradition, but we cannot assume that a hypothetical longer version would make any clearer to us what is going on. The whole poem is a mystery, but a mystery very specific in its elements. Presumably it bears some close connection to pre-Christian beliefs, and we cannot be sure of its original significance. The stepmother-witch is a familiar figure from fairy-tales, but we can only guess at the way in which the serpent and the mackerel may have had previous meanings attached to them, both occult and sexual. And what is the force of the mackerel's refusal to be turned back into a human being? Certainly it is powerfully dramatic, in that it destroys our expectations of a symmetrical pattern. But it seems likely that for the original listeners of the ballad there was some motive or meaning to the refusal that we no longer know of.

Since we cannot know what is behind the ballad, we have to treat it as we treat Grimms' fairy-tales—as something wonderful and exciting in itself, but which can tell us things about our lives in indirect terms only. And, as in the fairy-tales, images and narrative move us even though we do not understand their original force. It makes a completely satisfying whole as we have it, yet it is filled with mystery : the directness of utterance, the seeming arbitrariness of the narrative, the brutality of the action, suggest primitive forces that must remain interesting to us, because they are involved historically with the beginnings of civilization and psychologically with the beginnings of ourselves.

Omission, then, whether of incident, of motive, or of a whole social and religious context, is an important characteristic of most ballads as we have them. However the omissions originated, they result in an atmosphere charged with mystery: we are given bare situations, but of such intensity that their implications are very wide.

Mystery, I am aware, is a tricky word. A spurious mystery is easy to create. But it goes without saying that a ballad that survives for many generations is likely to be hard and solid through its very survival. The mysteries it contains are likely to imply something of importance to the ballad-singer and his audience, even though they might find it hard to explain.

The difficulty for a writer, for a poet sitting before his bit of paper, is to introduce such mysteries without his making them either into mere mystifications (and thus melodramatic), or into mere puzzles (and thus incomprehensible).

There are plenty of examples of the former. In fact the whole Gothic novel was founded on the supposition that mystification is the same as mystery. Hardy has plenty of such melodramatic mystifications—the wonder is not in the number of these, but rather in the number of times he managed instead to grasp the genuine savage central mysteries of the old ballads. But there are also occasions where the poem can, by creating ballad expectations which it doesn't fulfil, merely degenerate into a puzzle. A rather good example of the latter occurs in 'The Interloper', a poem Hardy published in the same volume as 'Who's in the Next Room?', which it resembles in pattern. We are first shown three people driving in a chaise and are told that they are accompanied by a mysterious fourth. But 'No: it's not anybody you think of,' we are told. Now we are shown other scenes, two of the people are in a cottage and then at a dinner party—the presence is still with them. Even if we had not read 'Who's in the Next Room?', the pattern and the omissions lead us to expect the extra presence to be that of Death, as Hardy is well aware, for twice again he tells us that it is not. All he lets us know at the end is:

> It is that under which best lives corrode;
> Would, would it could not be there!

There is no tradition for identifying it, and what Hardy tells us is far too general to be of much use—my own guess, remembering certain poems by Blake, would be, I think, that the presence is that of Jealousy. But I am wrong: for Hardy showed the poem to a

friend and the friend was perplexed, and as a result Hardy added
an epigraph when he reprinted the poem: 'And I saw the figure and
visage of Madness seeking for a home.'[1] Fair enough, but the information, coming in this way before the start of the poem, is
given too soon. The poem should move toward such information,
not in the light of it. With the epigraph, there is no mystery, and
without it, there is only mystification.

III

I would now like to read[2] a poem in which, while it is wholly
Hardy's own, the strengths and potentials of the ballad are more
completely and energetically used than in perhaps anything else he
wrote. What is more, as I hope to show, the genuine ballad mystery
is its lifeblood.

During Wind and Rain

They sing their dearest songs—
He, she, all of them—yea,
Treble and tenor and bass,
    And one to play;
With the candles mooning each face . . .
    Ah, no; the years O!
How the sick leaves reel down in throngs!

They clear the creeping moss—
Elders and juniors—aye,
Making the pathways neat
    And the garden gay;
And they build a shady seat . . .
    Ah, no; the years, the years;
See, the white storm birds wing across!

They are blithely breakfasting all—
Men and maidens—yea,

[1] Evelyn Hardy, *Thomas Hardy, a Critical Biography*, London, 1954,
p. 273.
[2] 'Hardy and the Ballads' was originally the Bain-Swiggett lecture given
at Princeton University in 1970. [Ed.]

CRITICISM

Under the summer tree,
    With a glimpse of the bay,
While pet fowl come to the knee . . .
    Ah, no; the years O!
And the rotten rose is ript from the wall.

They change to a high new house,
    He, she, all of them—aye,
Clocks and carpets and chairs
    On the lawn all day,
And brightest things that are theirs . . .
    Ah, no; the years, the years;
Down their carved names the rain-drop ploughs.

The first stanza firmly establishes the pattern, and it is a very
detailed one. Most of each stanza consists of a picture showing the
activity of what seems to be a growing family. We never know
at any point how many there are in the family, and that is not
important, but the activities show them in harmony—in the first
stanza literally in musical harmony. The vagueness about their
number is clearly deliberate, and contrasts with the precision of
observation that shows elsewhere. 'Treble and tenor and bass/And
one to play' or 'The candles mooning each face'—that is, the light
does not completely illumine, like the sun or an electric lamp; it
illumines only what is directly in its path, and leaves other surfaces
in a clear-cut shadow. The second stanza shows them all in a
different kind of activity—clearing moss from the pathways, an
occupation similar to that of burning couch grass, a quiet clearing
of space in nature so as to make room for human assertions. In the
third stanza the activity is of breakfasting out of doors—again
there is specificity where it is needed to make the picture clear
('With a glimpse of the bay'), and a lack of it where it is not needed
—we still do not know how many there are in the family now,
though it sounds as if it is still growing. And we do not know
exactly what the pet fowl are. But the generalness of the family
and the generalness of the pet fowl are part of the same point—for
the family's harmony is based on certain general rhythms of life
which are also those of birds and animals. This takes me three-
quarters of the way through the poem, but I have still not described
it all. Each picture of activity is cut short by 'ah, no' and an

exclamation about 'the years', for the scenes are pictures from the past, and they are being recalled 'during wind and rain', and each final line consists of an image from the present, an image of the natural destructiveness of the storm. 'How the sick leaves reel down in throngs.'—'See, the white storm-birds wing across.'—'The rotten rose is ript from the wall.' The language is suggestive, pictorial, and ominous. As contrasted to the ordered and harmonious health and ease of the family at their music, the leaves 'throng', they are sick, they go through a drunken dance of death. The movement is slow, the final lines being packed with difficult consonants, so that we cannot read them very quickly, and in one of them there is also a heavy alliteration. What is more, these lines rhyme with the first lines in the stanzas, separated quite as much as joined by the five intervening lines, and separation is also the point of 'ah, no', the words immediately preceding; for this set of images is a complete denial of the other set describing the family.

We have the pattern then: a contrast between past and present through two sets of images, and we have a loose narrative progression in the first set (those to do with the family). Comment is *implied*, only, by a certain complexity in the juxtapositions between the two sets. For the disturbing fact is that if we find the rhythms of the busy and burgeoning family to be 'natural' ones, we have to admit that the rhythms of the storm denying them are equally natural.

And so we come to the last stanza, which superficially seems to follow exactly the same pattern. The first image, of the family, is once again of lighted, airy, spacious activity, but the tone is here deceptive. They are moving house:

> Clocks and carpets and chairs
> On the lawn all day,
> And brightest things that are theirs.

It is an extraordinary picture, suggesting highlights on polished wood and clockface in the open sunlight. But wait—the first line was 'They change to a *high* new house', and the high new house might be the outdoors itself. All the circumstances are omitted, we are not told how or why their furniture should be left *all day* out of doors (though it seems to me possible that they are being evicted). Whatever is happening, it is odd enough to constitute a strong hint that the pattern is broken, the harmony is only apparent, and the family is in some way ended: and the mystery is all the greater in that the scene is as bright and airy as the other scenes that came before it, yet it may be the start of tragedy. As usual, it is followed by the denial, because even this scene is lost in the past, but it is in this stanza that the two sets of images (those to do with the family and those to do with the storm) come closest together in their import. The image from the past is bright, and the image from the present is dark, but the first implies calamity, and the second is of annihilation. And, in this final line, for the first time the image from the present refers directly to the remembered family:

> Down their carved names the rain-drop ploughs.

'Ploughs' suggests not only the movement of a rain-drop in a furrow, but also its obliterating action. Time and the elements are actually beginning to wipe out even their names and memories: the storm of the present is merely a most destructive embodiment of time and its inevitable process of ruin and denial.[1]

I would like to suggest that the strength of this poem is directly related to the presence of the three kinds of ballad-omission that I referred to. First in the narrative: there is even less linking of narrative than in 'Sir Patrick Spens'; instead there is a loose progression, for what we are given is a series of scenes which we must link for ourselves. Secondly there are the omissions of motive and character: we are never told the circumstances of the family, even the approximate number of people in it, nor is there any differentiation made between its members, and we are not given any reason for their 'change' in the last stanza. The third kind of omission is made too, though it is far the most difficult for a modern writer to manage, and it succeeds largely because of the way Hardy has managed the two other kinds—there is an almost complete omission of social and historical context, and what remains is there in

[1] My interpretation might be challenged by a reference to Evelyn Hardy's and Robert Gittings's edition of Emma Hardy's *Some Recollections*, London, 1961. 'The "high new house" of stanza four seems to be Bedford Terrace, to which the Giffords [Emma's family] moved,' say the editors. I would agree that thoughts about his wife's family were probably the 'source' of Hardy's poem, but a work is not the same as its source, and I have come across other readers who feel that something more ominous than a mere change of house is happening in the first lines of this stanza.

primitive simplicity without any false naivety. The family amounts to an emblem of human fruitfulness, of the whole of human life as it should be—but, amazingly, it is done without portentousness. On the contrary, Hardy presents it with clarity and modesty: we believe in the family first and only later realize how inclusive is its presentation. The emerged mystery is the subject of the poem: life in memory coexistent with death in the present. And though the poem is far from being a direct imitation of a ballad, the Ballads have been indispensable to its writing, and it is almost inconceivable without them.

IV

The ballad is the chief native source of our literature, and it remains a body of poems that has been constantly drawn upon as a means of renewal. For the Elizabethans the original Ballads were still a live form, and we have extracts from current ballads in Elizabethan and Jacobean plays, and sophisticated, clearly 'authored' ballads like the patriotic ballads of Drayton or the anonymous 'Tom o' Bedlam'. By the eighteenth century the ballad seemed an escape into the exotic from a literature that appeared to have become over-polite and over-urbane. In the nineteenth century it influenced in some sense almost every poet of importance. And in the twentieth the form has been at least tried out by many poets from Pound onward. At present it is probably more healthy as a living and popular form than at any time in the last two hundred years: most obviously in the ballads of Bob Dylan; but the Beatles' 'Eleanor Rigby' is a perfect urban equivalent of the traditional ballad, and Robert Hunter's words for the Grateful Dead or Robbie Robertson's for the Band are good ballads and good poems by any standard.

The traditional ballad, in fact, being a source, contains material enough for endless drafts and is not only the indirect source for most of the short poems in English literature, but the direct and conscious source for poems as different as a song by Shakespeare, a song by Blake, the Lucy poems, 'The Ancient Mariner', 'The Lady of Shallot', 'Who's in the Next Room?', 'Miss Gee', and 'The Ballad of Hattie Carroll'. The writers of different times may be searching for different things, but they can find them, or think they find them, in the ballad.

Josephine Miles has examined very brilliantly how the ballad has been used as a means of renewal. In the eighteenth century she finds it 'blurred' with Spenser to become part of the eighteenth-century 'sublimity'. On the other hand, she says,

> in the nineteenth and twentieth centuries there was a strong urge away from epic and epic scope and upholstery, toward depth, delicacy, and implication. And here again, other forces in the ballad seemed to serve: not its lords and ladies of high degree this time, but rather its quick and implicative narrative style, which got rid of adjectives in favour of verbs, let objects do the work of persons, and saw persons in basic family relation and in basic simple confrontation.[1]

I need scarcely point out how aptly all that Miss Miles says here applies to Hardy. She is not, in this passage, speaking of him, but it reads like a description of 'During Wind and Rain'. (Though I would still insist that if the urges away from and toward are common to Hardy and other nineteenth-century poets, he goes about them in a different way from any of his contemporaries.)

The characteristic of Hardy's poetry that seems to place it most firmly among that of his contemporaries is that it is narrative poetry. One of the major concerns of Victorian poets was to find a modern substitute for the epic, whether in longer attempts like the *Idylls of the King* or *The Ring and the Book*, or in shorter narratives—and certainly one way in which they tried to find it was through ballads. There is, too, a temptation to think of Hardy as a novelistic poet, but I would suggest that, though some poems are, as we shall see, novelistic in presentation, we think of him so because we are remembering that he did not start publishing books of poetry until he had published almost the last of his many novels. Though in truth, as Donald Davidson showed, the novels themselves derived from ballads. Such poems as 'Who's in the Next Room?' or 'During the Wind and Rain' go back to the same sources as *Far from the Madding Crowd* or *Tess*. There is a single-mindedness in Hardy's attachment to the Ballads—even though he may have made nineteenth- and twentieth-century emphases in them—that is greater than that of any of his contemporaries. Without their ballads and ballad-influenced poems there would still

[1] Josephine Miles, *Eras and Modes in English Poetry* (second edition), Berkeley, 1964, p. 108.

remain a major part of Browning's or Tennyson's work, let alone Swinburne's, Arnold's, or Hopkins's. But without such poems there would be practically nothing of Hardy's poetry left, and I hope to show how the influence of the Ballads continues even into his most personal poems.

I am convinced that all good writing (as well as some bad) is the product of obsession. Hardy's mastering obsession, in his prose as well as in his poetry, was a regret for the past. I would call it nostalgia if the word didn't imply something enervating. On the contrary it was the source of his strength—that is, the strength of his best poetry, and of the ideas most powerfully realized in it. Not the didactically presented ideas, the Pessimism, but the ideas implicit in and inseparable from such a poem as 'During Wind and Rain'. In any case it is incontestable that a large majority of his poems deal with a calling up of the past, usually combined with a regret for its passing, whether it is a public past (as in the ballads to do with the Napoleonic wars), or private (as in the poems of 1912–13 about his first wife), or a kind of combination of the two (as in 'During Wind and Rain').

There is a poem of his called 'Old Furniture', two stanzas of which sum up his feeling about the past in much of its complexity:

> I see the hands of the generations
>> That owned each shiny familiar thing
> In play on its knobs and indentations
>> And with its ancient fashioning
>>> Still dallying:
>
> Hands behind hands, growing paler and paler,
>> As in a mirror a candle-flame
> Shows images of itself, each frailer
>> As it recedes, though the eye may frame
>>> Its shape the same.

He was prepared to follow those frail images, those hands behind hands, for their own sake, but also as means of defining the present. Surely there has been no poet, even in medieval or Elizabethan times, who was more obsessed with the fact that the important and vivid Now slides immediately into the past, 'First memory, then oblivion's swallowing sea' ('The To-Be-Forgotten'). We live in the present, but we are conscious creatures, and we are weighed down by memories, which are all partial losses, and which will one day become total losses. He records not as 'a momentary stay against confusion' but as a momentary stay against loss. And there is a poignancy running right through his most robust poetry from the knowledge that it *is* only momentary.

For the poetry is almost always robust, never fretful or neurotic. He particularly records his own losses as only important because they are a part of other people's losses. It is never the poetry of personality : nothing could be further from him than the Confessional poetry that was all the rage in the US and England a few years back. He must have been a genuinely modest man. His first person speaks as a sample human being, with little personality displayed and with no claims for uniqueness—with as little distinguishing him beyond his subject matter, in fact, as distinguishes the personages of the Ballads beyond their actions.

V

So he was obsessed by the past, and he finds the Ballads (and forms derived from them) the perfect repository for his laments about passing time. To sum up Hardy's poetry as 'laments for the past' may seem to be rather limiting it, but after all a lot of the poetry most firmly enduring from the last three thousand years consists of exactly that. And as I have tried to show, the feeling of his poems is often one of a *general* regret : the family in 'During Wind and Rain' may have been a family he knew, it may not, but in any case the poem works for us as an evocation of possibilities which are now no longer possibilities.

But of course he was not confined to such general laments. I say of course because nowadays Hardy's best-known poems are probably those to do with *personal* loss, the poems of 1913 about his first wife. I would like to take now a poem that is not one of this group, but which certainly seems to deal with an incident from Hardy's own past and is immediately less generalized in theme than those I have discussed so far.

Near Lanivet, 1872

There was a stunted handpost just on the crest,
    Only a few feet high :

She was tired, and we stopped in the twilight-time for her rest,
    At the crossways close thereby.

She leant back, being so weary, against its stem,
    And laid her arms on its own,
Each open palm stretched out to each end of them,
    Her sad face sideways thrown.

Her white-clothed form at this dim-lit cease of day
    Made her look as one crucified
In my gaze at her from the midst of the dusty way,
    And hurriedly 'Don't,' I cried.

I do not think she heard. Loosing thence she said,
    As she stepped forth ready to go,
'I am rested now.—Something strange came into my head:
    I wish I had not leant so!'

And wordless we moved onward down from the hill
    In the west cloud's murked obscure,
And looking back we could see the handpost still
    In the solitude of the moor.

'It struck her too,' I thought, for as if afraid
    She heavily breathed as we trailed;
Till she said, 'I did not think how 'twould look in the shade,
    When I leant there like one nailed.'

I, lightly: 'There's nothing in it. For *you*, anyhow!'
    —'O I know there is not,' said she . . .
'Yet I wonder . . . If no one is bodily crucified now,
    In spirit one may be!'

And we dragged on and on, while we seemed to see
    In the running of Time's far glass
Her crucified, as she had wondered if she might be
    Some day.—Alas, alas!

This is an anecdote, and is aiming at something very different from
the other poems we have looked at so far—a circumstantiality, a

uniqueness of the remembered incident. The dated title suggests that we are to treat it as a bit of autobiography, but we would do so anyway—the oddness of the incident and the prosaicness of most of the style, in combination with the depth of feeling, would be enough.

For all the verse form, which with its alternating short and long lines slightly resembles ballad-metre, it is less like a ballad than the other poems discussed. It is something like an incident from a novel, but nevertheless the ballad hovers over it, and certainly Hardy is still making use of some of the ballad's great lessons.

The first is in the narrator's sense of himself. He is almost completely impersonal. The girl's emotion emerges quite explicitly, in her speech, but the man's is largely implied: first, by the fact that he should remember something so apparently trivial, and secondly by the poem's movement—until the last line. He is participant as well as narrator, certainly, but he is essentially the first-person participant of the Ballads, the general man, not different or special like the Romantic narrator nor obliquely boasting about the extremity of his emotions like the Confessional narrator, but experiencing the feeling any sensitive man would feel in his place.

Until the last two words of the poem.—And here we have the omission, the great implicative lacuna, which carries the full force of emotion hitherto held in, and which it seems to me is related to the omissions of the Ballads. We have the presaging of the metaphorical crucifixion, then simply 'Alas, alas!' A lot has been left out, but we do not need to know any more. It is like Sir Patrick Spens's misgivings followed by the image of the cork-heeled shoes. The worst fears have been justified, why go on?

There is another characteristic to the poem, however, and it is far from the Ballads—in fact it is close to the late nineteenth-century novel, Henry James's as well as Hardy's. There is what seems like a literal transcription of the fragmentary and incomplete speech and emotion. The speech is hesitant and interrupted, like real speech. I have mentioned that the style is at times prosaic—such an effect is deliberate, and part of the poem's effect. We labour into the poem, indeed. The first line is:

There was a stunted handpost just on the crest.

Hardly mellifluous writing. What is more, in spite of the naturalistic rendering of the speech, in spite of the prosaic patches, there are also certain phrases (all ending lines and thus needed for rhymes) which I can only call Hardyisms: 'dim-lit cease of day', 'the west cloud's murked obscure', and 'the running of Time's far glass'. Peculiar and uneuphonious, and close to poetic cliché. There is an awkwardness to such phrases that F. R Leavis has remarked remind us in their amateurishness of the Poet's Corner in some provincial newspaper.

This brings up the whole question of awkwardness in Hardy's poetry. It is of two kinds: the deliberate and the inadvertent. Poems like 'Who's in the Next Room?' and 'During Wind and Rain' contain little awkwardness of style, but they are (like the best poems of many poets) not quite typical of Hardy's work as a whole, which is marked by peculiarities of diction, metre, and structure.

There is a famous passage in his notebooks, dated 1875. He is speaking of prose-writing, but it is clear how it applies to (and comes from) his thinking about poetry:

> The whole secret of a living style and the difference between it and a dead style, lies in not having too much style—being—in fact, a little careless, or rather seeming to be, here and there. It brings wonderful life into the writing....
>
> Otherwise your style is like worn half-pence—all the fresh images rounded off by rubbing, and no crispness or movement at all.
>
> It is, of course [he is speaking of prose-writing], simply a carrying into prose the knowledge I have acquired in poetry—the inexact rhymes and rhythms now and then are far more pleasing than correct ones.[1]

There is a certain naivety to these remarks, and indeed they could be rather dangerous advice if taken literally. You can imagine someone writing his poem and then deliberately roughing it up a bit. And you recall Kenneth Rexroth's remark: 'There is always something a little synthetic about Hardy's rugged verse. The smooth [poems] seem more natural somehow.'[2]

I have said that Hardy doesn't strike me as a very Victorian poet, but of course no one can be completely outside his time, and we

[1] Quoted in Florence Emily Hardy, *The Early Life of Thomas Hardy*, London, 1928, p. 138.
[2] Kenneth Rexroth, *Introduction to Selected Poems of D. H. Lawrence*, New York (Viking Press), 1959, p. 2.

have to realize that though so much of his poetry is different from that of his contemporaries, he is with them in reacting against Tennysonian mellifluity—in fact he is with Hopkins and Bridges rather than with Swinburne. They are reacting against such writing as:

> And on a sudden, lo, the level lake
> And the long glories of the winter moon.

These are beautiful lines—on the whole too beautiful. We think more about the liquid 'l's than of water or moonlight. At the same time it's worth noting that the first line of 'Near Lanivet' is a barbarous kind of reaction: in 'there was a stunted handpost just on the crest', we think more of the 'st' sounds than of the lovers labouring up the hill.

The word to stress in Hardy's prose note is 'life' ('it brings wonderful life into the writing'). Hardy, for all his mournfulness, is mournful because he delights in the particulars of the present as much as a William Carlos Williams, but unlike Williams he can see their loss impending even as he delights in them. The particulars may be slight and ephemeral, but he records them with precision and vividness:

> The rain imprinted the step's wet shine
> With target-circles that quivered and crossed.

or, elsewhere:

> The twigs of the birch imprint the December sky
> Like branching veins upon a thin old hand.

If these two images are not positively uneuphonious, they are not that elegant-sounding either. But why should we care? They present things with immediate authority. Hardy's poetry is crammed with such images. It is one of the great pleasures of reading it that we are likely to come across them at the most unexpected moments.

Hardy's awkwardness, whether completely deliberate or inadvertent or even a funny mixture, comes from a concern for authenticity. It usually succeeds when his stylistic concern is subordinated to his concern for exact depiction of his subject. (Not surprisingly, you could say the same of Tennyson.) Rexroth's criticism is on the whole just, though there are exceptions to it. And I think 'Near

Lanivet' as a complete poem is such an exception. The poem is full of oddities, but those that do not succeed are small ones, and those that do are part of what is after all a pretty odd incident. A better statement of Hardy's conscious aesthetic would be his own sentence when speaking of Tess Durbeyfield's face: 'It was the touch of the imperfect upon the intended perfect that gave the sweetness, because it was that which gave the humanity.' His poetry is never as smooth as Tennyson's or Campion's but the small imperfections have their own sweetness when they are a genuine part of his subject-matter, because they indicate a faithfulness to its humanity.

VI

It may seem by now that I am overpressing my point. There is no question that Hardy was influenced by the Ballads. 'Near Lanivet' has the Ballads hovering behind it, even though it is a personal poem containing touches of novelistic technique. Like the Ballads, the poem narrates a presaging and like them it jumps across the way in which it has been actually fulfilled. And even here Hardy does not enter the poem as anything like an individualized character. But you might say that there are many other personal poems by Hardy, and that many of them—the famous poems of 1912–13, for instance—show little resemblance to the ballad. You might further go on to wonder what influence the ballad, a narrative form after all, could be said to have on the following lines:

> No shade of pinnacle or tree or tower,
>   While earth endures,
> Will fall on my mound and within the hour
>   Steal on to yours:
> One robin never haunt our two green covertures.
> ('In Death Divided')

Don't such lines, you might properly ask, bear even more resemblance to some seventeenth-century poem, some poem like Lord Herbert's 'Elegy Over a Tomb'?

I would like to return to the early ballads for a moment. No question, there is writing in Hardy that seems to have nothing to do with the strict definition of the ballad. But there is in the ballad too. James Reeves has remarked that it is impossible 'to draw a hard-and-fast line between ballads and folk songs, though such a line is often assumed.'[1] And there is the curious case of the lovely ballad known as 'Walsinghame' : this is a poem some believe to be by Sir Walter Ralegh, some believe to be an earlier ballad simply transcribed by him and so found among his papers, and some believe to be an earlier ballad partly rewritten by him.

> As you came from the holy land
>   Of Walsinghame
> Met you not with my true love
>   By the way as you came?

> How shall I know your true love
>   That have met many one
> As I went to the holy land
>   That have come, that have gone?

This is the genuine note of the ballad (one, incidentally, that Ralegh was perfectly capable of capturing) : I need only refer to the abrupt entrance into the poem by dialogue between unidentified speakers, the suggestion of mystery coming from different kinds of omission, the dramatic tone, and so on. The dialogue continues for a bit, and then the poem stays with one of the voices:

> Know that love is a careless child
>   And forgets promise past,
> He is blind, he is deaf when he list
>   And in faith never fast.

> His desire is a dureless content
>   And a trustless joy
> He is won with a world of despair
>   And is lost with a toy.

> Of women kind such indeed is the love
>   Or the word love abused
> Under which many childish desires
>   And conceits are excused.

[1] *The Everlasting Circle*, ed. James Reeves, London, 1960, p. 17.

But true Love is a durable fire
In the mind ever burning;
Never sick, never old, never dead,
From itself never turning.

This, on the other hand, is the note of many sixteenth- and seventeenth-century lyrics. The idea of love as a child, obviously Cupid, is Petrarchan, but the child is described in non-Petrarchan, one might say pre-Petrarchan terms. The reflections are direct and passionate, but impersonal. The speaker is certainly not individualized in the way that the speaker of 'The Canonization' is. Nevertheless, the note of these stanzas *is* found in certain poems by Donne, it is found often in Ben Jonson, and it is found in a host of other poems of the time. Yet, interestingly enough, this poem holds together: there is no inconsistency felt between the note of the ballad at the beginning and the note of passionate reflection at the end.

Rather, there is an essential consistency. Such a fact suggests that the reflective lyric, as found in English from Wyatt until well into the seventeenth century, was a natural development from the Ballads. The Ballads are a narrative form, but their economical style, the impersonality of the narrator, the musical intention, and the mystery and deep feeling of their subject matter, were all easily adapted to the reflective content of the second half of 'Walsinghame'. And Hardy, writing ballads all his life, but often turning to poems of reflection, naturally entered into a similar style—even though he seems to have admired such writers as Shelley and Swinburne, who wrote entirely differently.

I do not want to suggest a new orthodoxy. There are too many great traditions already. But it does seem to me that the related family lines of the ballad and the reflective lyric, joined by ties of economy and impersonality, have run permanently through English literature as providing in some sense a style that is always available. For their very neutrality and adaptability to new content, they have remained possible styles for about five hundred years, while other and equally impressive modes have been born, reached maturity, and died. The reflective mode I am speaking of is, as I emphasize, essentially impersonal, essentially non-confessional. It is concerned with its subject to the extent of excluding the speaker's personality, even when his emotion is the subject of the poem (as it often is)—for he sees his emotion as one which anybody in his situation would be able to feel. How better to exemplify this than from the poems of 1912–13, in which Hardy wrote of the loss of his first wife?

I'd like to start by taking two poems related in subject but not in style, 'The Haunter' and 'The Voice'. 'The Haunter' is rather close to the ballad as such, being spoken by the ghost of a woman, who is haunting the husband who cannot perceive her. It is an original but simple device that immediately suggests great complexities— the fact that she cannot communicate with him but wants to, and the fact that he knows it, corresponds to a common enough situation in human relationships and almost certainly to that of the Hardys' marriage in its later years.

> Now that he goes and wants me with him
> More than he used to do,
> Never he sees my faithful phantom
> Though he speaks thereto.

The wistfulness is not merely that of fantasy, then: their lack of contact is only a more permanent and more poignant version of the lack of contact they had toward the end of her life. The poem is light in tone—the double rhymes may have something to do with it, but there is besides a lightness to her speech, almost a childishness, almost a playfulness ('What a good haunter I am, O tell him,' she says, and 'Hover and hover a few feet from him'), as if being a ghost relieved her from too consistent a pain. But, as in the best of the old ballads, the adult agonies are fully implied.

Immediately after it in the *Collected Poems* comes 'The Voice', now one of Hardy's best-known poems. This is a companion piece to the other: it is Hardy's own attempt to see that ghost, to recapture that distant past view of her 'even to the original air-blue gown', and about his inability to do so. Stylistically it makes a complete contrast to the other: where 'The Haunter' was light and song-like, with accurate but unremarkable language, with a gentle tone in which deeper feeling was all implied, 'The Voice' is compressed, is suited to the speaking rather than the singing voice, proceeds very unsmoothly, and reveals a depth of personal feeling greater than in any other single poem of Hardy's. In reading it aloud, you have to pay attention to the variations of the movement, the anapaestic lines tending to slow and delay more and more, and eventually breaking into a completely different metre. Leavis has written brilliantly on this poem, pointing out how the difficult and at times odd language and the equally difficult movement perform a discovery of the speaker's feeling. The evocation the poem makes is very real, but it is less of the woman than of his present need for her—not as she was at the end of her life but as she was when they first knew each other. At the end, the feeling is as distinct and as individualized as in any poem by Hardy:

> Thus I : faltering forward,
> Leaves around me falling,
> Wind oozing thin through the thorn from norward,
> And the woman calling.

The agony of loss implied in 'The Haunter' is here explicit. In saying all this, I am setting the poem (with perhaps 'Near Lanivet') somewhat apart from the majority of Hardy's successful poems. The 'rugged' quality (to use Rexroth's word) here is what makes the poem the success it is, it completely authenticates the experience, in a sense : it bears no relation to the ballad or to the reflective lyric deriving from it. It is an exceptional poem by any standard, a real invention.

The other poem I wish to take from this group is the short one entitled 'The Walk', which contrasts with both. (These three poems, if there were no others by Hardy, would amply demonstrate the range and variety of his greatness—a range his critics have not much emphasized.)

> You did not walk with me
> Of late to the hill-top tree
> By the gated ways,
> As in earlier days;
> You were weak and lame.
> So you never came,
> And I went alone, and I did not mind,
> Not thinking of you as left behind.
>
> I went up there today
> Just in the former way;
> Surveyed around
> The familiar ground

> By myself again:
> What difference then?
> Only that underlying sense
> Of the look of a room on returning thence.

Like 'In Time of "The Breaking of Nations" ', it is a poem that at first reading seems almost too simple to make its point. It deals, with a deceptive calmness and gentleness of tone, with what you could call the trivia of loss. Yet in such trivia the whole of loss may be contained. The image at the end is almost casual, almost flat, almost not there, it is so commonplace. Yet, after all, it is precisely and terribly there, terribly because it is part of everybody's daily experience. There is no drama, no ghost: only the acknowledgement of a loss you have to live with, as everybody has to live with his losses—and it is as ordinary as a room. The style is bare and direct, it compresses a long period of experience and of attempts to come to terms with experience, into sixteen lines. R. P. Blackmur describes it, happily, as 'reduced to riches'. It is obviously unlike 'The Voice', but if 'The Haunter' is one of the culminations of Hardy's ballad poems, 'The Walk' is the culmination of his reflective poems. It is not about a unique experience, it is restrained but the restraint is a form of the attempt to come to terms with deep feeling, it has all the directness of the other poems I have called reflective lyrics. There are obvious differences between it and the second half of 'Walsinghame', but they are in the same tradition.

And we never for a moment doubt that Hardy means what he says. We make much of 'sincerity' nowadays—it is the most striking quality in the poetry of for example Allen Ginsberg or Anne Sexton. And clearly sincerity is a value, even though one rather difficult to define—maybe it is one of the ultimate values in literature. But there are different ways of being sincere, and I suggest that Hardy's is a supremely successful one.

The critics who have written on Hardy's poetry spend an inordinate time in complaining about the badness of his bad poems. The bad poems are certainly there, but though they may be boring or ridiculous they are never pretentious. By contrast, if you take the collected Yeats, you feel the strain of all that rhetorical striving in the minor poems, and it is only in the best of Yeats, and not always then, that he is able to free himself from the rhetoric. Rhetoric is a form of pretence, of making something appear bigger or more important than you know it is. Well, you never feel, even in Hardy's most boring and ridiculous poetry, that he is pretending—he is never rhetorical. And there are not many poets of whom this can be said. If the price paid for his fifty best poems is some hundreds of bad ones, it is well paid. And throughout, there is always the feeling that he is trying to see things as they are, whether it is an abstract term like Pity or a physical thing like the way the heat of noon breathes out from old walls at midnight; he is never trying to falsify either them or his emotion about them—and so much the worse if the poem ends up in bathos or flatness. Ezra Pound more than once praises Hardy for his insistence on immersing himself in his subject. And this is well said, for the immersion leaves him no room for pretence, or for anything other than honesty. Much of what sustains me through the flatter parts of the *Collected Poems* is this feeling of contact with an honest man who will never lie to me.

The honesty is related, I think, to a reticence. Clearly he was a man of exceptional reticence and modesty, and it seems as though it was necessary for him to embody these personal qualities in the impersonal narrator of the ballads and the equally impersonal reflective speaker of the other poems. It is a happy embodiment.

BEN JONSON

I

There are many Ben Jonsons to be found in this selection,[1] and each of them is a considerable poet. The poems here range from the vernacular patter of the songs by Father Christmas or the Gypsy to the formality of the 'Hymn to Diana', from the most savage epigrams to the tenderness of the epitaphs or small elegies on dead children, from Petrarchan conceits to the severity of 'Though beauty be the mark of praise'. I have to stop, or I would go on for another page pairing the extremes between which he moves so easily. All I can do here is to comment on a few of his poems and try to describe the kind of pattern they create for me when they are put side by side.

His poetry (as apart from his plays) has always been surprisingly neglected, considering its variety, and surely one reason for the neglect in the last century and a half is that so much of it can be damned as 'occasional'. That is, much of it is elicited by external events, or is intended to compliment some noble, or is written to commend another person's book. And nowadays we tend to use the phrase 'occasional poetry' to indicate trivial or insincere writing.

Yet in fact all poetry is occasional: whether the occasion is an external event like a birthday or a declaration of war, whether it is an occasion of the imagination, or whether it is in some sort of combination of the two. (After all, the external may lead to the internal occasions.) The occasion in all cases—literal or imaginary—

---

[1] First published as the Introduction to the author's Penguin selection of Ben Jonson's verse. [Ed.]

106

is the starting point, only, of a poem, but it should be a starting point to which the poet must in some sense stay true. The truer he is to it, the closer he sticks to what for him is its authenticity, the more he will be able to draw from it in the adventures that it produces, adventures that consist of the experience of writing.

I would like first to point to one of Jonson's poems most clearly occasioned by an external event, the 'Epitaph on Master Vincent Corbet'. It is probably not one of the poems that sticks out on a first reading of Jonson's poetry, it is modest and at first sight rather conventional. The beginning is indeed formulary, though there is a tranquil sweetness of tone that accords well with the sweetness of nature in the man lamented. The emotion, perhaps, is more of admiration and respect than of love; admiration and respect for a life that was 'all order, and Disposure'. Jonson, like so many of his contemporaries, looked up to the moral chastity of someone who *knew* what was right to do (and did it) rather than having to learn it from experience. ('Not to know vice at all, and keepe true state,/ Is vertue, and not Fate', he says in another poem.) 'Disposure': his admiration is also for the willed, conscious, rational *arrangement* of a life. Arrangement as in a garden (the nurseries of the mind):

> His Mind as pure, and neatly kept,
> As were his Nourceries; and swept
> So of uncleannesse, or offence,
> That never came ill odour thence:
> And adde his Actions unto these,
> They were as specious as his Trees.

The poem, though still lucidly written, concentrates here to a statement of some weight. For the arrangement that he admires is not one of counters, of fixed things, but of living qualities like plants in that they grow, need tending, encouragement, pruning, and have a past and a future of change. This gardener is the opposite to Candide, for his garden involves him in the essentials of life, is a type of experience and not a withdrawal from it, and may result in actions that are as 'specious' (splendid) as trees.

At this point in the poem there is a return from the figure of the garden to plain description, but description that shades into rather complex interpretation of its subject:

> 'Tis true, he could not reprehend;
> His very Manners taught t'amend,

They were so even, grave, and holy;
No stubbornnesse so stiffe, nor folly
To licence ever was so light,
As twice to trespasse in his sight,
His lookes would so correct it, when
It chid the vice, yet not the Men.

That the last line is translated from Martial is perhaps a fact of larger importance for Jonson than it is for me. Whatever its source (and 'sources' are sometimes a bit like 'occasions') it emerges as a kind of discovery, the product of an exploration performed with a quietness and pertinacity suitable to its subject-matter. After this passage the poem, it seems to me, returns to formula once more, but the formula is meant seriously, you could say it is being re-experienced—for if the last few lines afford no surprises, they are certainly not slip-shod.

From this I'd like to turn to two far more ambitious poems, 'To Penshurst' and 'To Sir Robert Wroth'. These also seem to be 'occasional' in the conventional sense, in that they were written for specific people or families (in fact it looks as though they started as thank-you letters). They also are direct and plain in style; what figurative language they contain is far from startling. Yet for all the plainness of statement, both poems are full of small vivid touches that contribute a certain richness of detail, as when Jonson refers to 'some cool, *courteous* shade' or tells of hearing 'the loud stag *speake*'. Such detail suggests a kind of bounteousness to the noble estates he is describing. There is besides some pleasant classicizing in both, and some versions incorporated from Juvenal and Martial. In both poems, also, the verse movement has a variety within firmness that conducts the reader with great ease through the descriptive passages, giving such description the liveliness of comment.

About line 35 of the first poem, we realize that Penshurst is a kind of English Eden. Moreover, it is not based on guilt; here again is the admiration of chastity:

And though thy walls be of the countrey stone,
They'are rear'd with no mans ruine, no mans grone.

The poem to Wroth goes into even more detail about what he has avoided, for he has never wanted

To blow up orphanes, widdowes, and their states;
And thinke his power doth equall *Fates.*

Both poems are about the responsibilities of rank, the second concentrating on the moral responsibilities, the first on the social. The
'Sylvanes' and the translated bits from the classics are not mere
decorations but are functional references to a moral and social
tradition that Jonson sees continued from classical Rome to Jacobean
England. In fact, 'To Penshurst' tells us far more about the Renaissance views on rank than many histories or literary commentaries,
as Jonson leads us from tenant to guest (the author himself) to the
final anecdote about King James, which is told with such grace and
ease that for the while it gives a certain dignity even to that cold
and pompous man.

However, the coolness, the formality, the eschewing of any
striking rhetorical techniques, the general sense of external occasion
dominating the poem, the suspicion that Jonson is just trying to
please the gentry, make a modern reader find such poems—initially
anyway—almost distasteful. But I would suggest that the poem
explores values that are genuinely Jonson's and genuinely those
of his hosts, and that Jonson takes it as a matter of course that they
are shared. It is difficult to put oneself into a time when admiration
for rank was not snobbery, but we have to make the attempt, and
if we can do so then we have a chance of understanding the ideas
that Jonson is trying to embody in these poems. As to the lack of
showiness in the style, it is clearly deliberate, and is an attempt to
further realize the Eden-like chastity of those values he is exploring
so carefully. The Eden is not a garden of primitive luxuriance but
a seventeenth-century garden 'all order, and Disposure', and the style
is of a piece with it.

II

These two poems are successful attempts at English classicism, both
in derivation and in invention. They have moreover the smoothness,
control and urbanity that we associate with 'classical' writing. It is
interesting that most of those who have succeeded best in writing
so, i.e. within restraints both technical and passional, have been
people most tempted toward personal anarchy. For them, there is

some purpose in the close limits, and there is something to restrain.

Certainly there is also a wild anarchic vigour in Jonson, but unlike the kind of classicist I have just mentioned, he permitted himself to use it, and use it with wonderful success, as anybody who has seen the plays will recollect. And he was besides a master of rhetoric, in both the modern sense of rhetoric as showiness, and in the old and more neutral sense of rhetoric as that sum of devices necessary for persuading the reader.

Probably Jonson started his writing career by writing the additional scenes to Kyd's *Spanish Tragedy*, and he continued to try every 'style' he could, not feeling bound to stick with one and develop only within it. The critics had not yet begun encouraging writers to identify style with personality, and to move with stately idiosyncrasy through Early, Middle, and Late Periods that could be mistaken for nobody else's. Indeed, you may find an exuberant early-looking style and a sober late-looking style jostling each other in consecutive works by Jonson. 'Her Triumph' (from 'A Celebration of Charis') is probably a product of his middle age, for example, and it is as lush a poem as ever came out of Elizabethan or Jacobean England.

I have been in danger, so far, of overemphasizing the chaste and classical Jonson, and perhaps oversimplifying him. In the first of the Epigrams he exhorts the reader to 'understand' his book, which in the context of so much plain writing does not look difficult. But even with the Epigrams Jonson clearly means the process of understanding to be more than the business of merely comprehending the text. He is probably the best epigrammatist in English because he does not intend his statements to be light commendations or dismissals, but witticisms (however elegant) placed in the context of a society's whole experience. Understanding means taking them to heart, means—ultimately—*acting* on them.

But understanding becomes something far more difficult when we reach the baroque works like 'Eupheme', the 'Elegie on the Lady Jane Pawlet', and 'To the Immortall Memorie, and Friendship, of that Noble Paire, Sir Lucius Cary, and Sir H. Morison'. Quiller-Couch, evidently, found the opening of the last so bizarre that he omitted the whole first half of the ode in his *Oxford Book of English Verse*. And it is difficult to us still, the difficulty being one of tone—even though we have the advantage of greater familiarity with the tonal ambiguities of Jonson's contemporaries than most late Victorians had. The anecdote about the infant of Saguntum was evidently considered appropriate to a serious poem, but it does not accord with our ideas of decorum. The difference between the seventeenth-century attitude and ours on this matter is rather similar to the difference in attitude towards puns. We find puns a form of forced and infantile humour, whereas they found them elegant and rather beautiful, like ingenious rhymes.

The difficulties of tone are less easy to abridge out of the 'Elegie on the Lady Jane Pawlet', which many a modern reader would accuse of ludicrous elaboration and insincerity. And I think to read it properly we have to make a far more rigorous effort to think like seventeenth-century people than we did with the 'Epitaph on Master Vincent Corbet' or 'Her Triumph'. Earlier I used the word baroque, and used it seriously: for example I would ask the reader to think of paintings by Rubens (an almost exact contemporary of Jonson's), the large ladies of the court being judged by an elegantly dressed Paris, or being improbably wafted up to an apotheosis by angels as fleshy as they are—going to God's court with the same kind of pomp as they would to that of James I. What we must remember is that artifice is not necessarily the antithesis of sincerity.

Perhaps it is relevant here to quote from Christopher Isherwood's definition of High Camp, a term he invented. His character says: 'true High Camp always has an underlying seriousness. You can't camp about something you don't take seriously. You're not making fun of it; you're making fun out of it. You're expressing what's basically serious to you in terms of fun and artifice and elegance' (*The World in the Evening*). And we can assume that the fun and artifice and elegance of the 'Elegie on the Lady Jane Pawlet' were considered by Jonson's contemporaries to be an essential part of what must have seemed a splendidly moving public compliment.

The poem begins as dramatically as anything by Donne. Jonson pretends ignorance of the ghost's identity but obeys her summons: 'You seeme a faire one!' Then he recognizes her, and his exclamations would be positively melodramatic if they were not so exquisitely modulated by the flexibility, the continuous life, of the verse movement. He is almost stone, he is in fact marble, it seems, and a marble breast is an appropriate enough place for Fame to inscribe the Lady Jane's epitaph ('it is a *large* faire table', he says half-ruefully, he of the 'mountaine belly'). He is thus led to the apt inscription of her name and title in the poem. After a summary of her virtues, there follows the elaborate and beautiful description of her fatal illness and death. The elaboration is the beauty, the beauty the elaboration. She becomes a martyr, her soul addressing the doctors:

> 'Tis but a body which you can torment,
> And I, into the world, all Soule, was sent!

The scene takes on the ceremoniousness of a court masque as she makes her exemplary farewells,

> And, in her last act, taught the Standers-by,
> With admiration, and applause to die!

It is total artifice, as in Rubens. Jonson then conducts her into a seventeenth-century heaven, and exhorts her parents:

> Goe now, her happy Parents, and be sad,
> If you not understand, what Child you had.
> If you dare grudge at Heaven, and repent
> T'have paid againe a blessing was but lent,
> And trusted so, as it deposited lay
> At pleasure, to be call'd for, every day!

He continues and ends the poem with an evocation of the Christian's certainty of entering Heaven, and even here there is the same hyperbolic and 'staged' feel to the verse, from the detail of 'the Starres, that are the Jewels of the Night', to the exultant ease of movement in the last few lines, where the Christian

> Gets above Death, and Sinne,
> And, sure of Heaven, rides triumphing in.

To those who are repelled by the artifice as such, it might be worth pointing out that 'Her Triumph', which many generations have found so immediately satisfying, is hardly a *realistic* poem either. In it, Charis is drawn in a car by swans and doves, and the whole thing is full of hyperbolic compliment and stagey artifice. Where the 'Elegie' differs is that moral precepts and also wit come into it, and most of us are as ill-equipped to deal with such a combination as we are to appreciate Shakespeare's puns. Besides, it is another 'occasional' poem, though I would suggest that (unlike the 'Epitaph on Master Vincent Corbet') the occasion is largely one of Jonson's imagination.

III

The 'Elegie' and 'To Penshurst', in their different ways, both come from Jonson's public self, something that it is important to understand in Jonson as it is not in, say, Donne or Herbert. It was not a public self like Byron's or Robert Frost's—which were all personality, and personality, at that, drawn from the poems as if by a bad biographer. Certainly his personality, even his eccentricities, can be induced from the whole body of his poetry, but it can be done more because of the extent of the public exposure than because he made any deliberate display.

The public self appears in three roles in Jonson's poetry: as critic of literature and culture, as critic of society and morals, and as poet laureate (laureate either to the king, or, more loosely, to the nobility in general). The roles are not always distinct: you could say, for instance, that in 'To Penshurst' he combines all three. For his literary and cultural criticism is meant in the largest sense. He links the classicism of Sidney (as in the *Defence of Poesy* and the *Arcadia*) with the classicism of Pope (as in the *Epistles*): it is not merely a question of bringing Martial or Juvenal up to date, or even of building up a national literature that can rival the classics, it is a matter of continuing the life and society that was behind the literature, evaluating, adapting, naturalizing it. So in finding the Roman virtues in a Kentish estate he was acting simultaneously as a critic of literature and of society. And of course he was also acting as a kind of laureate to the Sidneys.

The public self, then, is probably what we first notice, as Jonson would have wanted, yet there is a fierce and intense private self within it, which accounts for many of the public self's virtues and which in quite a few poems has an independent life of its own. Some of the poems are openly personal, and in others the personal emotion enters, you feel, almost in spite of his intentions.

The least interesting of such poems are those of spleen and bitterness—I have not included in this selection the poems against Inigo Jones, or the completely nasty 'Answer to Alexander Gill'. But I have included the revealing 'Odes to Himselfe', which are somewhat similar to each other in many ways. The one he wrote on the failure of *The New Inne* is better in detail than in its scheme, which fails to convince me. The feeling in the poem is of total contempt and of badly disguised fear. The public are swine, and feed like swine; dramatists are posturers. The imagery is powerful—it is of filth, mould, rottenness, and stale sweat. Behind it is the revealed but unacknowledged fear that the public might just be right in having rejected his play, and that his mind might be following his bedridden body into helplessness. The remedy at the end, to 'sing/ The glories of my King', though elegantly written, lacks the power of the invective that comes before it.

The other 'Ode to Himselfe' is better in all ways. It is somewhat less abusive (the public here consists of small fish rather than of swine), and there is a greater dignity to the action proposed at the end—something we can believe in as a possible course for Jonson instead of the hyperbolic wishful thinking that came at the end of the other poem.

> And since our Daintie age,
>   Cannot indure reproofe,
> Make not thy selfe a Page,
> To that strumpet the Stage,
>   But sing high and aloofe,
> Safe from the wolves black jaw, and the dull Asses hoofe.

Two lines taken from his own *Poetaster*, and well worth taking.

Yet aloofness was not always easy to achieve, and we might question whether the classical aloofness of the statue or the star is such a permanently desirable position to take up. It is comparable to the chastity of him who is virtuous because he does not 'know vice at all'.

Certainly, as I have implied, such an aloofness or chastity was something Jonson admired because it was so difficult for him to achieve. He seems to have been torn betwen partial love and partial hatred for the world and himself. I suppose it is the tornness that he does so well, the fact that he is prepared to follow through his hard doubts and try to find a few things that he can depend on. He is the tough tormented man who wrote the following in *Timber*, his collection of aphorisms:

> What a deale of cold busines doth a man mis-spend the better part of his life in! in scattering complements, tendring visits, gathering and venting newes, following Feasts and Playes, making a little winter-love in a darke corner.

There is a wistfulness in the last phrase that is also found in 'My Picture Left in Scotland':

> I'm sure my language to her, was as sweet,
>> And every close did meet
>> In sentence, of as subtile feet
>> As hath the youngest Hee,
> That sits in shadow of *Apollo's* tree,

he says there, his writing being an example, incidentally, of the poetry he is describing: it is all ease and sweetness, like a madrigal with its varied line-lengths and its re-echoing rhymes. 'Oh, but,' he exclaims, breaking the smoothness very simply by substituting a trochee (the first in the poem) for the expected iamb—and we get a clear-eyed look at himself, a fat man in middle age:

> Oh, but my conscious feares,
>> That flie my thoughts betweene,
>> Tell me that she hath seene
>> My hundred of gray haires,
>> Told seven and fortie years,
> Read so much wast, as she cannot imbrace
> My mountaine belly, and my rockie face,
> And all these through her eyes, have stopt her eares.

It is a simple poem, in a sense, but I have never come across another like it. The aloofness of mountain and rock is forced on him by age, and he frankly would prefer a little winter-love. It is a poem of self-pity, and (in spite of all that I was taught at Cambridge) self-pity is something people feel often enough for it to be a subject worth writing about. It is unusual here in that it is without either an admixture of self-hatred or an impulse towards special pleading: it is dignified, completely unwhining, circumstantial, and even at one point slightly funny ('she cannot imbrace/My mountaine belly').

The personal feeling here is of far greater complexity than that of either of the 'Odes to Himselfe', and is also of greater authenticity in that it is nowhere *willed*. The whole question of willed feeling comes up again, however, in 'To Heaven' and 'On my First Sonne'; in fact it is, in different ways, the subject of both poems.

'To Heaven' looks at first glance as if it were all argument, but it is all feeling in the way the argument is conducted. It starts with careful, slow, qualified statement, the verse movement suggesting the effort after precision. It speeds up in the ninth line:

> As thou art all, so be thou all to mee,
>> First, midst, and last, converted one, and three;
> My faith, my hope, my love: and in this state,
>> My judge, my witnesse, and my advocate.

There is an effort to get things straight; and the repetition of the familiar trinities reassures him, so that for a couple of lines the emotion emerges pure and intense:

> Dwell, dwell here still: O, being every-where,
>> How can I doubt to finde thee ever, here?

The rest of the poem in its paraphrasable content seems to support the confidence of these lines, but in the actual writing is the result of somewhat mixed emotion. Having had the assurance of God's care, he still has to return to the difficulties of life: he rehearses them wearily even while protesting that it is not weariness that elicits his love of God. Again, it is like no other poem I can think of: the feeling in it is controlled, admitted, denied (it seems), and then perhaps converted, and is conveyed at least as much in terms of the verse movement as those of the words; the movement, by shifts of a caesura and shifts in degree of stress, keeping the statements in a greater sense of uncertainty than the words themselves would indicate. (The uncertainty could be demonstrated at greater length by contrasting the movement of these couplets with the movement of those, say, that conclude 'To Penshurst'.)

Willed feeling is even more essentially the subject of 'On my First Sonne', in which he is casting about for ways in which to cope with his loss. The first four lines are gentle, and it is almost as if he is taking refuge from despair in learning and 'conceit'. 'Farewell, thou child of my right hand', he says, recalling the Hebrew sense of the name Benjamin. The conceit of the child as lent to its parents he uses also in the 'Elegie on the Lady Jane Pawlet', but here it is more bald, he is unable to play so amusingly with the familiar thought. And in line five the emotion breaks out (as it did in the middle of each of the last two poems I have described). 'O, could I loose [lose] all father, now.' He continues with questions that seem but are not rhetorical, questions he tries to still with another piece of ingenuity ('here doth lye/Ben. Jonson his best piece of poetrie'), which is at the same time fully felt, and ending with feeling that is neither easy nor ready-made, feeling about the dangers of feeling.

The emotions in these two poems are difficult, scrupulously created, and qualified : he cannot live with despair more than any man, but he also cannot pretend that willed equanimity is simple or constant. He was never more true to his occasions.

HOMOSEXUALITY IN
ROBERT DUNCAN'S
POETRY

An unusual article appeared in the August 1944 issue of Dwight Macdonald's monthly journal *Politics*. It was by Robert Duncan, described as 'a young poet who lives in New York City', and was entitled 'The Homosexual in Society'. Something of the complex eloquence of Duncan's later prose already shows up in his argument that the homosexual, and particularly the homosexual artist, accepts his separation from society too readily. Instead of refusing to be rejected, he lives in secrecy, narrows the scope of his sympathies, and cuts himself off from the wider concerns of, say, a Proust or a Melville. It was an unusual article in many ways, not least in suggesting that the homosexual should publicly identify himself as such. The author then proceeds to do just that, though aware of 'the hostility of society which I risk in making even the acknowledgement explicit in this statement.'

The hostility of society showed itself pretty soon. Duncan had previously submitted his long poem 'An African Elegy' to the *Kenyon Review*, whose editor, John Crowe Ransom, had accepted it enthusiastically in a letter discussing it at some length. But now, as a direct result of the article in *Politics*, Ransom refused to publish it. Looking through the early issues of the *Kenyon Review*, I find quite a few contributions by writers who were well known to be homosexual. But most of them were never to admit it in public, and Ransom's extraordinary complaint about Duncan was that he was indulging in something he called homosexual advertisement.[1]

[1] The correspondence between Duncan and Ransom is deposited in the Washington University Libraries, St Louis, Missouri.

It is well to remind ourselves how little precedent there was for Duncan's testimony at that time and in that society. Homosexuality was held in peculiar horror even by liberals who would not have dreamt of attacking other minorities. In the mid-fifties, when I asked my teacher and friend Yvor Winters why he did not like Whitman's poem about the twenty-eight young men bathing (*Song of Myself*, 11), he replied that the homosexual feeling of the poem was such that he could not get beyond it. (On the other hand, he was able to consider *Billy Budd* the great book that it is.) Homosexuality was even, in our lifetime, thought to be contagious : many educated people believed, at least until the first Kinsey report appeared, that a single sexual experience with a member of one's own sex was enough to alter the direction of one's inclinations for good.

Most homosexual writers until at least the 1960s dealt with autobiographical and personal material only indirectly. One method was for a poet to address his work to an unspecified 'you', giving an occasional ambiguous hint about what was really going on to those in the know only. (This is what Auden did, and what I was to do later.) Another method of indirection was to 'translate'—either to change the gender of a character into its opposite, in a play or novel, or by a less conscious procedure to do what Duncan admitted doing in earlier poems : in the past, he said in *Politics*, he had 'tried to sell [homosexual feelings] disguised, for instance, as conflicts rising from mystical sources'.

But from now on Duncan's homosexuality was a matter of public record. His early bravery found few imitators for many years. Meanwhile he had won himself an interesting artistic freedom : he could speak about his sexuality openly but with barely any twentieth-century tradition of such openness behind him. He had to create it for himself.

In the 1966 introduction to his selection from his early poems, *The Years as Catches*, Duncan raises the possibility that his sexual and poetic beginnings may be connected. 'Perhaps,' he says, 'the sexual irregularity underlay and led to the poetic.' The neutral word 'irregularity' suggests that the emerging consciousness, finding its desires out of harmony with those of the society around it, extends itself into a realm—that of art—where things are not judged by mere regularity, where the harmonies to be reckoned with are far

more comprehensive, and where one in fact aspires to the extraordinary—the *Divine Comedy*, *King Lear*, *Ulysses*.

But meanwhile he was exploring the irregularity, and its presentation was not a very happy one in these earliest poems, either before
or for some time after the article in *Politics*. He himself notes the
prevalence of images of disease in that early poetry, and suggests
Auden's most brilliant book, *The Orators*, as an influence. But they
are also the product of the normal romantic gloom of a young man
in his early twenties, deepened no doubt by the fact of a world war.
At one point even, in properly Keatsian tradition, he refers to himself as 'death-wedded'.

And there is indeed a disguising, as he says, or maybe a muddling,
of the sources of his conflicts. The figure of the lover in the earliest
poems has an alarming tendency to suddenly turn into Jesus—a Jesus
of the Hopkins brand, you might say. And when it is not grandly
religious the love-making in this poetry is something of a sterile
compulsion. As late as 1946, he begins a poem,

> Among my friends love is a great sorrow,

and later moves into the lines

> We stare back into our own faces.
> We have become our own realities.
> We seek to exhaust our lovelessness.

These are plain statements of deep feeling: their abruptness, their
parallelism, give them the sound of propositions, but they are propositions of ennui and despair. Nevertheless, love is already starting
to be his central theme, and he sees himself afterwards as already,
in such poems, preparing for 'the development of Eros and, eventually, for that domesticated or domesticating Love that governs the
creation of a Household and a lasting companionship'.

This is the year when he grows up as a poet. In the earliest poems
he had been somewhat at the mercy of his material, but from now
on the material is his, and he uses it as a secure home-base from
which he moves out into unexpected implications and extensions.
In the following year he wrote the complementary sets of poems,
Domestic Scenes and *Medieval Scenes*. There is talk of love, but it
is an unspecific and usually unsatisfied love. It is still a self-regarding
desire for love rather than an immersion in the real thing. In
Domestic Scenes everyday objects and situations—an electric iron,

a radio, a ride on a streetcar—are used as emblems of the heart. The feeling is sentimental and ironic. He is scared of getting off the bus at 'Reality Street', and later he says with a kind of worldly self-pity,

> I have playd the horses—Crucible,
> Nom de Plume, Ecstasy, and Werther.

As a current song has it in 1976, love is just another high.

If there was a deliberate self-limitation in subject-matter and mood in these poems, there is by contrast an opening up of both in the other group, *Medieval Scenes*. The poetry is still inhabited by the unhappy and deprived. But their sorrowings are bright and exquisite, there is rich invention and surprise of detail. The main theme is of separation, the inability of one to 'touch' another, at times the inability—even in this gorgeous and brocaded landscape— to get beyond the self at all, except maybe in sinister dreams. Inevitably these poems remind of visual arts: but the 'scenes' are static, as in tapestries or *tableaux vivants*. A whole court is frozen in a fixed attitude, elegant and brilliant, but with all energy to move, to touch, and to change mysteriously blocked.

> The splendid Emperor of Jerusalem dreams
> of the Emperor of Jerusalem in his splendor.
> The poets at their board
> subvert the empire with their sorrow.
> Powerless and melancholy, the young men smile
> evasively and stroll
> along the shores of the slumbering lake. We hear
> the diapasons of a drownd magnificence.

In the writing, however, he reaches beyond the langorous limits of the scene. It contains a secret energy, which points to possibilities beyond the subject-matter.

Yet anyone who first encountered Duncan through his later work—that is, the majority of his readers—can see that this particular mode, of the wonderfully embroidered tapestry, is not one that he sticks with. Having mastered it, he abandons it as too limited, too 'finished'. In 'I Tell of Love', of the following year, he turns to another kind of poem which (though I find the writing less startling than that of the *Medieval Scenes*) leads forward in style and subject to the maturity of *The Opening of the Field*. Like

Cavalcanti's 'Donna mi prega', on which it is a 'variation', it is about the fleshing of a god, the living presence of that god in the joining of two people. He transforms and re-creates their lives, for he is the very god that the young courtiers of Jerusalem were unable to conceive of. Duncan has returned from the sentimental ironies of *Domestic Scenes* and the pictorial objectivity of *Medieval Scenes* to the less defined, less distanced, more risky, more *personal* mode in which most of his best poetry has been composed. There is a sense, however, in which this particular poem can be seen as rather a statement of intention, a programme, than as a realization. Duncan strains to reach beyond the limits, to immerse himself in love, but if he does so here it is by an act of will.

I referred above to 'two people', because *homosexual* love is merely the occasion for a poem which would be just about the same if it were about the relation between a man and a woman. And this is the poet's point, surely : that love of one's own sex, just as much as love of the opposite sex, is the start of that training that reaches to the god's presence.

It is in 'The Venice Poem', also of 1948, that he is prepared to distinguish the characteristics of homosexual from heterosexual love. In the section beginning 'Accident will finally strip the king' he explores in particular the question of narcissism in the love of one's own sex. A man loving another man beholds somebody *like himself* :

> Nature barely provides for it.
> Men fuck men by audacity.
> Yet here the heart bounds
>   as if only here,
> here it might rest.

But this is only a short section of a long and complex poem in which there is little rest. If the poem is about the Venetian empire and the empire of poetry, it also explores fully the ambivalence of empire-building. The man approaches his lover,

> eager to love and yet
>   eager to thrive;
> so too his lover
> meets him,

> arrogant and alive, his eyes
>   seeing already
>   more than Love's mirror shows.

The lovers see more than Love's *mirror* shows, that is they are not lost in the depths of a mere narcissism; but they can also see more than *Love's* mirror shows—they are 'eager to thrive'. I think of the saying, 'A hard cock knows no conscience'.

Most of the severely experimental work between 'The Venice Poem' and *Caesar's Gate* (first version, 1955) is so impersonal that it contains little relevant to my theme, so I will pass over these years. Caesar's Gate takes up where my quotation from 'The Venice Poem' left off: it is dominated by the hard cock with no conscience. I spoke earlier of a secret energy in the style of *Medieval Scenes*. Here the energy is everywhere, and, emboldened by the experimentation of the intervening years, it informs an extraordinary book. It is about sexual hell, where lust is continuous, and where neither body, mind, nor spirit can be satisfied. In his 1972 preface to this book, Duncan speaks of how love, which can lead to the Household, the place of growth and harmony, also contains a fury. This work, then, largely focuses on sexual fury, both self-mastering and self-defeating. Afterwards he can see the hell as a place he had to pass through on the way to the Household, but at the time he can see nothing ahead. There is more than a little self-dramatization in the book, but it is appropriate, as it is in Baudelaire, in that it is an integral part of the subject revealed: indeed, self-dramatization is the distinguishing characteristic of this particular circle of hell.

There are reminders of other writers than Baudelaire: Duncan renders the punishments of the sexually obsessed in Dantesque terms. 'Torches, we light our way', one poem begins. Another finds the speaker as a kind of zombie, between living and dead: he says,

> O holy Dead,   it is the living
> not the Divine
> that I envy. Like you
> I cry to be rejoind to the living.

And there is the repeated image of the worm curled within an eye, a brain, or the world itself, much reminding me of Blake's worm in the crimson rose.

Action also takes place on the surface of the earth, which coexists with hell, each seen as it were through the transparency of the other. A pick-up tells him:

> If you fix your eyes upon my body
>   you will see
> I have no soul at all.

And in 'An Incubus',

> I . . . seize upon my own cock, hot with blood.

> Love, Love, the demon sighd
>   fitting his unflesh to my hunger.

I am reminded of Dante, Blake, even of Rimbaud, but rather of their concentration than of their mannerisms. If there is horror at the core of the book, I still feel delight in knowing that a man can render even horror with such memorable force.

But there is the difficulty of the poem 'H.M.S. Bearskin', with which Duncan tries to come to grips in his 1972 preface. Bearskin is an old queen, a stereotype, a kind of gay Stepin Fetchit. He lives in a world of self-caricature, of homosexual affectation and campiness which stylizes all that enters it into triviality. The poet positively sneers at him:

> Ridiculous, the butterfly,
> avatar of the serious worm,
> he lights upon the merde of Art,
> that swish old relic, self-enamourd
> fly-by-night, he hovers
> among the cafe tables.

This is characteristic of the writing in this short series-within-a-series: even though the butterfly-fly-worm imagery holds together neatly, the tone is uneasy and itself slightly hysterical. I can feel a little more comfortable with the Bearskin poems only by trying to invoke a historical sense. Twenty years ago, when homosexuals found it necessary to be much more secretive, many were forced into enclaves within society, little ghettoes. All ghettoes tend to stereotype behaviour, giving fixed styles to its eccentricity, as Duncan already knew in his article in *Politics*. Coming from a 'salon' in 1944 he remembers 'the rehearsal of unfeeling' that he found there, even in himself:

> Among those who should understand those emotions which society condemned, one found that the group language did not allow for any feeling at all other than this self-ridicule, this gaiety . . . a wave surging forward, breaking into laughter and then receding, leaving a wake of disillusionment, a disbelief that extended to oneself, to life itself.

Those of us who chose not to be part of such enclaves did however feel a certain sense of threat from the effusive stereotypes: they seemed to be *parodying* femininity. Were we in fact really like that ourselves, we wondered, if we just let ourselves go? Nowadays the thought that they could be a threat seems laughable; for the more a ghetto disperses itself into the surrounding society, the more various are the patterns of behaviour available to its members. But at the time the threat seemed real enough. And we hate what threatens us.

So I can certainly see how Bearskin has a place in Duncan's homosexual inferno of 1955, even though the writing of this section is uneasy and wavering, and both the feel of horror found elsewhere and really focused satire are absent.

Duncan speaks of Bearskin in his 1972 preface at some length, but here too he fails to convince me. (He even refers to 'harpies', like an outraged newspaper editorial. I wonder if I am a harpy.) The determinedly trivial person may indeed be destructive, but in the Bearskin poems as they stand without preface, Bearskin hardly strikes me, at least from this distance, as being 'an avatar' of the worm within the world.

The strength of *Caesar's Gate* is elsewhere, outside of this semi-social comment, when Duncan is speaking of the internal agonies. There is more to its strength than horror: in the midst of torment comes the voice of defiance,

> All facts deny the way,
> deny I love. Only I
>
>   remain to say
>   I love.
>
>   I say I love.

Men fuck men by audacity, he had said, and perhaps he has to pass through this hell not only as a price for the audacity but also as a test of it, in such a way that one can move beyond it. And certainly the characteristic mode of the book is one Duncan has put behind him: its dramatic and concentrated intensities contrast greatly with the quieter and even self-deprecating tone of the concluding poem added in 1972, a poem related to the rest of the book mainly through its metaphor of 'Asia', which lies on the other side of Caesar's Gate.

To move from the imitations of Gertrude Stein and the inferno of *Caesar's Gate* to the later books is like moving from a series of rooms into open country. The vision introduced by *The Opening of the Field* is the reverse of that in *Caesar's Gate*: it is open, inclusive, expansive. The Gate, he has explained, is the pass that prevents the conqueror from moving into Asia. Now he, the conqueror and empire-builder as poet, has moved through that gate into a larger territory that is indeed haunted, as he had heard it would be, but by spirits that mingle continuously with the living in mutually pleasing concourse. (The much later 'Passages 1, Tribal Memories' contains the following:

> For this is the company of the living
> and the poet's voice speaks from no
> crevice in the ground between
> mid-earth and underworld.)

The book can be seen, and was surely intended, as a single poem, each separate unit being part of the mesh (the mesh of Rime) and relating to every other unit. Thus an image may have many references: in 'The Structure of Rime I', Jacob wrestling with the angel is said to have 'wrestled with Sleep like a man reading a strong sentence'. Such references moreover may be taken up elsewhere in the book or in later work. One could point to the quoted line as a kind of model of what happens in this volume: there are multiplicities of meaning that one doesn't get to the end of easily. The ambiguities sometimes cluster very thick, but time after time Duncan's sense of direction draws him clear of what might have been only confusion, and the visions—of which after all the ambiguities are an essential part—emerge clearly from the very fogs that generated them.

Among the fields, plains and meadows of this book, 'The Place

Rumord To Have Been Sodom' is marked out with especial clarity. This is the poem that I think finally compensates for the apparent contempt in the Bearskin poems, by providing a context in which they can be retrospectively understood.

> It was measured by the Lord and found wanting,
> destroyd by the angels that inhabit longing.
> Surely this is Great Sodom where such cries
> as if men were birds flying up from the swamp
> ring in our ears, where such fears that were once
> desires walk, almost spectacular,
> stalking the desolate circles, red eyed.

It seems that Sodom had been inhabited by Bearskins, and others like them, and that God destroyed it as the younger Duncan would have liked to (in his own word) 'disown' them. But there is a Bearskin in everyone, and Duncan, or God, can never disown any part of himself. The place 'lies under fear' until one can understand that fear is part of the greater rhythm that is Love. (As in Dante, where Love rules many seemingly contradictory elements as part of its dominion.) The revelation is that

> *The world like Great Sodom lies under Love*
> *and knows not the hand of the Lord that moves.*

This is what 'the devout', 'these new friends', have learned, who 'have laid out gardens in the desert' that once was Sodom; this is what the original inhabitants were unable to learn. It is one of Duncan's best poems, echoing the note of the psalmist or of Blake's prophetic books, and moving with a sustained and sonorous rhetoric from the melancholy of the first part to the joyful sound of the last four lines:

> In the Lord Whom the friends have named at last Love
> the images and loves of the friends never die.
> This place rumord to have been Sodom is blessd
> in the Lord's eyes.

Elsewhere in *The Opening of the Field* there is comparatively little about the love of man for man. The vision of the book, like that of this poem, is larger than one of mere sexuality, though including it. And it is here Duncan establishes once for all that his muse is female. Female because it is the female who gives birth:

only from interaction between complementary opposites, the male poet and his female muse, can the real poem be born. (Where this leaves woman poets I am not sure.)

The muse then is fertile. And fertility is one of the main subjects of the book, the fertility of the field in its title: 'This is the Book of the Earth, the field of grass flourishing,' he says of a meadow but could equally well be saying of these poems. He sees 'evil' as a necessary part of the fertile process. In 'Out of the Black', Lucifer is in love with God. In 'Nor is the Past Pure', Kore is 'Queen of the Middenheap'—which is made of 'corrupted' materials. 'Corrupted' is a pun, evil is as necessary to the scheme of love as rotted stuff is necessary to the ecology of the meadow: 'Death is prerequisite to the growth of grass.' So the sterile loves are necessary to the emergence of the productive loves; so Sodom had to be destroyed to become blessed; and so the conquering poet had to stop in the hell at Caesar's Gate before he could enter the great fields of Asia.

I have proceeded chronologically so far, but it would be difficult to go on in the same way. Duncan's subjects become larger and more inclusive as he goes along, and it becomes steadily less easy to separate the sexual themes from the others. Certainly, homosexuality is as central to Duncan's poetry, to its origins and its realization, as it is to Marlowe's or Whitman's, whose work can hardly be discussed comprehensively without taking account of it. Yet, as I have implied, he is no more than they *merely* a Gay Poet, sexuality being only an important part of his whole subject-matter.

His whole subject-matter. Duncan's is poetry that discusses itself and its possibilities rather as the Chorus in *Henry V* discusses the possibilities of the stage he is standing on. In the mature Duncan— that is, in the work from *The Opening of the Field* onward—it discusses itself in such a way that its themes and subjects can be seen in continual interaction: sex, war, art, love, dream, language etc., and that is indeed his mastering subject, their interaction.

So I would like to abandon chonology, which is less useful in discussing the work of the matured poet, and concentrate on describing three figures or themes that recur in the next two books and in the scattered but plentiful work following them. I will call these figures—for they are human figures—the searcher, the mother and the lover.

The searcher is above all the adolescent and young man. He is seeking something out but its shape is still unclear to him. He was the author of the earliest poems, those of the first half of the 1940s. And he is the subject of the *Moly*[1] poems of 1971, in which Duncan is haunted by the ghost of himself at the age of fifteen. Spring is felt as a rage of expectancy to which the adolescent's rage contributes. The boy lives in 'the incompletion of desires', both longing for the fulfilment of simple lust and longing for that fulfilment to have meaning. He goes on the long random walks of adolescence looking for a someone, the ideal who is also on such a long searching walk, whose random wandering may suddenly intersect one's own, and whose needs would respond to one's own needs. So Proust wanders as a youth, hoping by chance to run across a girl from the village. The village girl is a provisional identity given to that abstract and unrealized someone, the raw outline of that Albertine whose space in his later life is already being opened up and made ready. But the need has to mature : the lover is not yet to be found.

> I was never there. He was never there.
> In some clearing before I reacht it
> or after I was gone   some *he*
> had laid him down to sleep where Pan
> under his winter sun had roused the wildness with his song,
> and, long lingering,
> the air was heavy with his absence there—
> Lord of the Heat of Noon still palpable
> where late shadows chill the dreaming sand.

He finds on his father's death

> an emptiness in which an absence I call *You*
> was present.

It is like an Old Testament prophecy of the Messiah who will some day occupy the readied space.

The adolescent is the perfect embodiment of the searcher, but the theme of sexual restlessness never completely leaves Duncan's poetry, as it never completely leaves the human being, however

---

[1] A group of six poems based on themes from Thom Gunn's *Moly* (1971) : *Poems from the Margins of Thom Gunn's Moly*, 'The Author's Typescript Edition' (250 copies), San Francisco, 1972. Reprinted in *Poetry Review* LXIII, 3, pp. 195–203. [Ed.]

harmonious the household he has in the end assisted in creating. In his nightmare form the searcher becomes the Frankenstein-like Prince of 'A Sequence of Poems for H.D.'s Birthday' (*Roots and Branches*), 'in his laboratory, assisted by the boy' who 'experimented in sensations'. But he is also the walker in the cities, walking more purposefully now. 'Night Scenes' from the same book starts with an evocation of the risk, flashy beauty, and headiness of walking the city by night:

> The moon's up-riding makes a line
> flowing out into lion's mane
> of traffic, of speeding lights.

The poem's images suggest the search for excitement, but already it is performed amongst larger patterns of meaning:

> Our nerves respond to the police-cars cruising
> a part of the old divine threat.

But the poem goes beyond: in the second part the innocent boy's orgasm is seen, simply, as lovely in itself, and in the third part the city is transformed to a woman, a mother containing men.

I have already pointed to some of the manifestations of this mother-goddess-muse in *The Opening of the Field*. And presumably in the twentieth century I don't have to explain the relevance of them to the title of this essay. But before coming to some of her later embodiments I should say something about the relation of dream to Duncan's poetic procedures. I have already mentioned the complex associationism of Duncan's work, particularly his later work. The procedure has been common in this century, and was perhaps first used thoroughgoingly by Pound in the early *Cantos*. Figure melts into figure, name into name, image into image. The ship carrying the kidnapped Bacchus is transformed into a kind of jungle-shrine to the god, vines tangling the cars, panthers padding round the decks. Helen of Troy becomes Eleanor of Aquitaine, both separate and individual women, but both manifestations of the same ideal figure.

The prototype of the experience of shifting identities is to be found in the dream, in which a friend may merge into one's cousin, who may in turn merge into some well-known political figure. Much of Duncan's poetry, particularly what he has published from 1960 onward, has been based on dreamwork. And by acknowledging the dream-basis to so much of his writing, he gives a peculiar right-ness and strength to the associationistic procedure. One person melts into another in the poem as he did in the dream, but never arbitrarily, because there is a rationale to the order of the most random-seeming dream, even though it may elude the dreamer.

A chief concern, then, of this later work, has been in the multiplying manifestations of the Mother: there appears, for example, Duncan's literal mother (whom he never saw) and his adopted mother, but these in turn relate to the ideal Mother, who is the muse and the principle of generation, and who is also the city, and who in one poem becomes in turn H.D. and Emily Dickinson. In 'Achilles' Song', she is the sea, the foetus's mother whose blood tides around him, both remote and near at hand, undefined because everywhere.

But in 'My Mother Would be a Falconress', from *Bending the Bow*, the mother appears as a distinct and close figure, no less mythical for her clarity. The images of her as Falconress and him as the obedient little falcon who is later to break away from her enable Duncan to dramatize the whole series of conflicts involving possessiveness and love on the one hand and freedom and the need for identity on the other. Every detail is strangely right, showing how his life is patterned by her contradictory demands: she holds him by the leash of her will, *but* she sends him out into the world on fierce errands, to kill the little birds, *but* he is to return with their bodies without eating them himself, *but* she rewards him with meat. Her ferocious love keeps him in her control by its very inconsistency.

> She lets me ride to the end of her curb
> where I fall back in anguish.
> I dread that she will cast me away,
> for I fall, I mis-take, I fail in her mission.

And the pattern that she has created is still retained. Years after her death, he still longs both to be her falcon and to go free. It is a startling poem both for what it is and for what it suggests. It suggests, for example, the ferocious Goddess who demands sacrifices as her due; and on the other hand it embodies a perfect example of what Gregory Bateson calls the double-bind (typically used by the mother) which he sees as the principal cause of a common type of schizophrenia. Yet these are only implied in the poem, where the mother is merely, completely herself, so living that she is impossible to deny.

This poem, too, originated in dream. A version of its first two lines came to him in sleep, as he records in the prefatory note. And at one point, he the falcon even dreams within the dream:

> I have gone back into my hooded silence,
> talking to myself and dropping off to sleep.

But there is a sharpness of focus to the poem that makes it unusual in Duncan, much of whose success elsewhere in his later work depends on the changing or even blurring of focus. I find it unprecedented in his poetry.

And then there is the male dream image: 'the shadowy figure' who appears in 'A New Poem':

> I would not be easy calling him
> the Master of Truth
> but Master he is of turning right and wrong

and

> He will not give me his name
> but I must give him . . .
>
> name after name I give him.

Ultimately he is a male counterpart to the Mother. But not an exact counterpart—rather than the Father he is the Lover. And the figure of the lover is as important in Duncan's poetry as is that of the mother-muse, though his is not a parallel function. (If I had to separate the functions of lover and mother I could say that he belongs more to the subject-matter of Duncan's poetry and she belongs more to its source. But it is far from a clean separation in a poetry that discusses its own sources so extensively.) He too merges identities, and changes form, function, and name as in a dream. But 'A New Poem' immediately precedes the first three 'Sonnets'.

The first of these is largely a translation of Dante's passage about Brunetto Latini, but it leads into Duncan's own comment:

> Sharpening their vision, Dante says, like a man
> seeking to thread a needle,
> They try the eyes of other men

> Towards that eye of the needle
>   Love has appointed there
> For a joining that is not easy.

This is a good example, incidentally, of the way in which Duncan takes over another man's work, extending an implication until it becomes his own. The threading of the needle is Dante's, but it is Duncan who extends the image into 'a joining that is not easy' (recalling 'Nature barely provides for it' of 1948). We are led immediately into 'Sonnet 2':

> For it is as if the thread of my life
>   had been wedded to the eye of its needle.

And then he shows us his lover putting together a patchwork quilt, joining the different colours and textures, the selected materials from past experience, into a covering for the shared bed. This is no dream: his lover is there, sitting near the speaker. And he is 'a worker', by this activity working in the shops of both art and love. He too works under the muse, then, and has, too, helped to create a household within her city.

Later this figure becomes dreamlike again: in the dance of 'Sonnet 5', he becomes a Platonic universal,

> a constant
> First Caller of the Dance
> Who moves me, First Partner, He
>   in Whom
> you are most you.

And later yet he returns in one of Duncan's most extraordinary and satisfying poems, 'Interrupted Forms'. I quote only the last few lines, but this does the poem something of an injustice, because the themes and experience presented in it braid together so tightly.

> I am speaking of a ghost
> the heart is glad to have return, of a room
> I have often been lonely in, of a desertion
> that remains even where I am most cherisht
> and surrounded by Love's company, of a form
> wholly fulfilling the course of my life interrupted,
> of a cold in the full warmth of the sunlight
> that seeks to come in close to your heart
>   for warmth.

It is used as a kind of prelude to the *Moly* poems, some of which also dealt with ghosts. The ghost of the lover in the past haunts the place where the lover still lives, 'interrupting' the life that is itself an interruption of 'inertia in feeling'. Love necessarily varies in intensity. And the Household is not the home of complacency.

The energy of the poem hovers between hesitations, much as a ghost hovers between being and non-being. But it is far from the self-dramatizing energy of *Caesar's Gate*, and the ghosts are far from the hysterical zombie who cries to be rejoined to the living. The poem is about the attempt to understand a complex and intense relationship. And it is primarily the work of a poet, of a homosexual poet only secondarily.

This is why I shall end here. I said earlier in this essay that Duncan started with little modern American precedent for speaking openly about homosexuality. There is now a way of speaking about it, and we may thank Duncan's continued example more than any other that it is not a specialized speech, it is not separated from the heterosexual's tradition. It is due more to Duncan than to any other single poet that modern American poetry, in all its inclusiveness, can deal with overtly homosexual material so much as a matter of course—not as something perverse or eccentric or morbid, but as evidence of the many available ways in which people live their lives, of the many available ways in which people love or fail to love.

NEW LINEAMENTS

Florida East Coast Champion, by Rod Taylor, Straight Arrow
Books.

The earlier part of Rod Taylor's first book shows him adventuring
both toward and from identity. In 'Crossing', for example, he
moves across the continent away from his Florida self and toward
a California self. But here and in other early poems, the movement
is more *from* than *toward*. In his restless poetic exploration of
North America, Taylor becomes numerous from his numerous
sharings in the experience of others. Much in the tradition of Walt
Whitman and Bob Dylan, who are clearly important to him. Images
of auto, train, and radio recur because they are means of travel,
they connect one man to all other parts of his continent. In fact,
'San Francisco Connection' is the punning title of one of his most
beautiful poems, and all of it takes place inside a car. And in
another poem, about the radio, he says,

> My fingers on the knob, working to crack
> a public safe, move
> through thousands of miles,
> many lives . . .

He also explores another dimension with something of the same
effect, running time backwards and 'becoming unborn'. He does so,
not for mystical purposes, but as a means of returning to his own
and American origins. From the dedication onward his book em-
phasizes the family and forebears. Again, the exploration of time,
like that of space, risks the loss of the individual self, the ego: but

by taking such a risk he can extend the sympathies of the consciousness.

There is a third way in which such sympathies may become extended and the identity become diminished or lost, and this is the way with which most writers are familiar, that of the imagination. A novelist, for example, has to 'become unborn', if only for a short spell, to participate in the lives of his characters. And in poetry one of the ways in which the imaginer typically transcends his single life is in the use of metaphor:

> It is here. It is now. It is time
> and I know it as a tree knows the time
> to let the colors of earth
> and sun blaze up in its leaves, or as a weasel
> knows the hour
> to be like snow.

The passage is characteristic of Taylor's writing: we understand at once, though the thought is complex and original; the perceptions are incorporated with swiftness and energy; and they are such that they extend the single self to share imaginatively in alien experiences.

But the poem from which these lines come, 'Lighteater', is not only one of the best, it is also the most disturbing in the book. It is about a kind of freak-out in which the consciousness watches itself dying, and in which the sense of identity is abandoned so completely that its chief components—the brain and words—are in the process of being lost: Taylor at this point learns, in terror and desperation, that his self-preservation both as a poet and as a man has depended on the health of his brain and its words.

So the second half of the book consists, in a sense, of an attempt to go back and rebuild the identity, starting at the beginning and going forward in time. The title poem, 'Florida East Coast Champion', is a twenty-one part autobiography; not the most promising or interesting project for a poet in his early twenties, you'd think, but the work is a triumph. He comes cunningly to the autobiography, spilling himself into existence in the second section, called 'Rain':

> It is blood
> of owls and lynxes storming
> on the roof, blowing through

the screen door, and it pours
like I poured out of noplace
on the Old Dominion, entering all
bodies living or not
because it has to.

It is still not the idiosyncratic self (as in Lowell) that Taylor writes of, nor the ego in its pride (as in Yeats), but what you might call 'geographic self', for his attempt is to define and 'place' the self in terms of sharable experience—and experience, in particular, as it arises out of specific locality. His feeling is never slack: though his subject is himself, he is never self-regarding: he looks outward, and feeds on the world. He scoops life far and near into his poetry, not recklessly but with the discriminations of someone who experiences so fully that he is sensitive to relevance.

The last lines of the section called 'Dream Animal' show the kind of richness that can result from such discriminations:

teach me to run
where I need to, through straining
roots, among rock, my nerve-trees billowing up
in the unlocked animal blood
on fire with the genius of instinct.

That's it, he has grasped the two sources of strength: he perceives 'the genius of instinct', and he perceives that a large part of human health depends on verbal health. Each perception guards over the other, helping instinct to become verbal, helping the words to find their source and power in something pre-verbal, as in the quoted lines. The language in them is doing rather more than trace the lineaments of life: it has something of the power of those lineaments themselves, going beyond anything we can literally speak of as metaphor into something very close to what Roethke called 'the anguish of concreteness'.

For me, Rod Taylor is simply the best poet to turn up in the last fifteen years. His poetry is the real thing: it is not the partial poetry I read a lot of the time and often in a rather qualified way admire (since it may after all do some things well), but whole poetry, in which the writer is fully living, he holds back no reserves.

IMMERSIONS

In the Distance, by Dick Davis, Anvil Press Poetry.

This book does not force itself on your attention. When I first read it, I thought: Well, that's nice. But I read it again, and then again, as things from it returned to my mind and I went back to confirm them. I began to realize that these poems will probably still be with me in ten years' time, and there are not many recent books of poetry I can say that about.

Dick Davis's discourse is quiet but insistent. It helps that he means what he says, that he is not too polite. He has a bold mind and imagination.

Here is a short example of the kind of poem that you almost pass over on a first reading. It is called 'Narcissus' Grove'.

> A place for the evasive, self-lockt stare,
> The useless beauty that the world disowns:
>
> Water sedulous over the grey stones—
> The pines' sweet resin scents the sleeping air.

That seems simple enough. But then you read it again, and the statement becomes less clear-cut, less of a statement perhaps. You pause at the cool daring of the metrical substitutions in the third line, the almost but not necessarily human suggestions of 'sedulous' and 'sleeping', the increasing ambiguity of the second pair of lines in relation to the first. The scene contained in it is complete in itself, adequate, reminding you a bit of Whitman's animals, 'placid and self-contained'; but the more you think about it the more perplexing is the connection, and lack of connection, between words like 'evasive' and 'sedulous'. And that's what the poem is about; it

138

isn't merely a muddle. In his four lines Davis has presented a mystery, and by presenting has not solved but intensified it. Both 'experience' and 'statement' are here, but not in exact relation : the experience does not simply illustrate the statement, nor does the statement explain the experience. Both go beyond each other, vexingly, wonderfully, as they do in our lives.

Davis's other poems explore similar or different patterns made between experience and meaning. But when I say patterns I do not mean to imply that he withdraws, that they are *merely* patterns. On the contrary, his typical image for the giving of self to experience is of immersion. In the brilliant early poem that starts the book, 'The Diver', a man sinks from the known day to the bottom of the sea and, confronting the treasure-wreck, 'hesitates, then/ Wreathes his body in'. It is an action of total involvement. Similarly the art historian, when he seems to others at his most pedantic, immersed in the minutiae of his study, 'is desolate with love'. Only by such a complete giving of oneself to experience, for its own sake not for its meaning, can meaning be properly pursued.

And there is the constant use of images to do with sleep and dream, being the types of self-immersion. Moreover in dreams we find incident loaded with meaning that is not quite revealed. Some of the poems about waking states carry dreamlike feeling too. In one of the most striking poems of the book, 'Scavenging after a Battle', the scavenger is left with 'colour cupped in his hand' just as his own figure is cupped by the surrounding landscape. Every image contributes to a cold, fresh strangeness. The scene is presented physically and cleanly, but an unstated significance hovers around the edges.

Unexplained significance is the characteristic not only of dreams but of myths. Thus Actaeon, lost anachronistically among 'eucalyptus trails', sees Diana as if she were a hallucination, but feels the bite of her dogs '*through* the dream'. The Virgin Mary is oppressed by the very folds of her clothes. And 'Jesus on the Water', infinite, realizing 'that no specific/Can contain my stare', observes how

>   . . . my feet tread water
> Only, as a stare
>
> That blurs particulars
> In tears.

The interinvolvement of abstraction and particulars is both the subject and the method of these lines.

In some of the poems experience awaits meaning and it does not come—'Desire' and 'North-west Passage' are two of the harshest poems in the book. In another, 'Childhood', experience awaits, and the waiting, the tentativeness, the expectancy, are the subject. Here is the whole poem:

> Imperceptible, at sunrise, the slight
> Breeze stirs the dreaming boy, till silently
> He edges free from sleep and takes the kite,
> Huge on his shoulders like an angel's wings,
> To climb the hill beyond the drowsing city.
> Released, the first ungainly waverings
>
> Are guided out, above the still valley,
> Constrained to one smooth flow, diminishing
> Until the pacing boy can hardly see
> The dark dot shift against the constant blue:
> He squats and stares: in his hand the taut string
> Tugs, strains—as if there were still more to do.

I don't need to refer again to immersion or dream. It is as if the boy is led on by his own sense of luck, trusting in the intermittent but renewed pull. That pull is like the verse movement which leads us similarly to the last line where, as in the best of Davis's poems, it doesn't quite work out exactly, it isn't pat. 'As if there were still more to do'—a slight resemblance to E. A. Robinson here is forgotten in the gentle urgency of the feeling. For Robinson the line would signify possibilities neglected—but here it looks forward, mysteriously, beyond the end of the poem. It is the wind that powers the poem, that stirs, guides, constrains, tugs, and in the end suggests that there is still more to do. And the wind's imperative is something compelling and recognized but insubstantial and unformulable. (Ezra Pound: 'This wind is held in gauze curtains . . .'; 'No wind is the king's . . .'.)

Experience is unformulable, and human beings have an uncontrollable urge to formulate. The paradox is old but basic, and it occurs throughout the book, both in the poet and in his subject-matter. Poem adds to poem, the book is a marvellous accumulation, complex, complete.

It is a first book, but a very mature one. The style is firm, totally without pretension, but all art. The majority of poems are metrical: at a time when most American poets consider metre obsolete and most English poets who use it do so as if it *were* obsolete, it is wonderful to find a poet (English) whose poetry lives through its metre. His handling of it is masterful, and you are never aware of effort. And the language is exact but relentless, like the perceptions. On the basis of this book, I would say that Davis is one of the best poets around.

A HEROIC ENTERPRISE

─────────────────⌘─────────────────

Divine Comedies, by James Merrill, Atheneum.

Mirabell: Books of Number, by James Merrill, Atheneum.

I feel rather as if I were setting out to review *Ulysses* in 1922. 'The Book of Ephraim' is a ninety-page poem from the volume *Divine Comedies* (1976), and *Mirabell* is its book-length sequel, published in 1978. (A third and concluding part will come out in 1980.) It is not that they are so difficult to understand as that they are so unprecedented, their ambitions are so high, the relationships both to each other and to the rest of Merrill's work are so complex.

James Merrill is one of the few members of that generation of poets from the 1950s who still writes in rhyme and metre. Most of the rest converted to free verse once and for all in the early 1960s, and inveighed against their previous metrical misdeeds with the uncompromising energy of old sinners who have seen the light in the barracks of the Salvation Army. Out of such testimony arose the curious phrase 'naked poetry'. Of course, Merrill, like any good poet, had never used metre and rhyme as if they were clothes that could be put on or off the naked body of his meaning. They were part of that body.

His poetry was as personal, in its way, as Ginsberg's—it too was about travels, family, male lovers, friends. And while the impulsive life of Ginsberg has been exposed to us through an impulsive style, improvisatory and unrevised, the elegant life of Merrill was presented in an elegant style, witty and punning, in rhymed stanzas or grouped sonnets. It was elegant, again, not like clothing, but like the behaviour—the manner and movement and gesture—of the body itself.

If style is an instrument of exploration, Merrill's developed into a most precise instrument. He explored certain aspects of his childhood through seven run-together sonnets in his well-known poem 'The Broken Home' of 1967. It is an honest but disturbing poem: it answers all the questions it can about the past and candidly leaves open those it can't. One of the questions left open is that of the distance between 'I' in the present and 'I' in the past. There is an odd reserve in the portrayal of his adult self: we are told more about what he does not do and what he is not than about what he does and is; and dealing with the adult first person was to be a recurring problem, I think a conscious one, for Merrill in his poetry of the 1960s and early 1970s. His poetry has been, typically, personal and anecdotal, but the narrator was most comfortable as an almost anonymous observer (as in the very funny 'Charles on Fire'), least comfortable at the centre of the poem, where on occasion (as in 'Days of 1964') the treatment becomes positively rhetorical. The rhetoric amounts to a kind of withholding, but I am not sure of what.

A writer goes from good to better by acquiring a grasp over new kinds of material. The material may well have been there, in the writer's life, for a long time, but the grasp is a matter of being able to accommodate it in the imaginative life of his writing. The advance in 'Ephraim' is striking. The shorter poems had dealt with marvellous fragments of a sociable life—a rather grand one, as sociable lives go. The two parts of the trilogy present a 'world' as complete, as foreign, as inclusive and as detailed as those of Mann in the Joseph books and of Tolkien.

It turns out that Merrill and David Jackson, the man he lives with, had for twenty years been communicating with spirits on a ouija board, and with one especially, an affable familiar called Ephraim, who had been a courtier on Tiberius's Capri, where he was strangled at the Emperor's order for having had sex with the young Caligula.

Much of the conversation is about the transmigration of souls, which pass through many bodies, and Merrill and Jackson speak with other spirits (the dead between bodies) including those of two recently dead friends, one famous and one not: W. H. Auden and Maria Mitsotáki (who was the subject of an earlier short poem).

The sessions at the board are set against the domestic and social life of the two men over a period of twenty years. Not only against this, though. During these years Merrill was attempting to transform the accumulating mass of fascinating material into a novel. Ephraim disapproves of the novel, as involving too great a transformation of the facts, amounting to a falsification; Merrill describes it amusingly and perhaps unfairly as weighed down with crude symbolic meanings; eventually his subconscious enables him to lose the troublesome manuscript in a taxi.

In his novel of 1965, *The (Diblos) Notebook*, Merrill had tried to discuss the process of writing a work of fiction while actually writing it, but 'Ephraim' is even more complicated: not only does he discuss the poem while writing the poem, he also discusses the lost novel. And so we have fictional characters, living and dead, rubbing shoulders with real characters, living and dead. Extremely complex relationships, need I say, are built up.

The poem is discontinuous, in a sense. It is divided into twenty-six parts, arranged in chronological order, but each a separate poem with its own thematic organization. The style varies in pace and density. Merrill has never before been so eloquent and so lucid: he speaks, for example, of how 'power's worst abusers' (Hitler or Caligula) are held 'incommunicado' after death, their souls not for re-use, 'cysts in the tissue of eternity'. At another point he refers to a spirit 'in whose mouth the least/Dull fact had shone of old, a wetted pebble'. The succinct but almost laconic force of such metaphor is the fruit of some twenty-five years or more of writing.

Merrill's attitude to his 'sources', the voices from the other world, is disarmingly open-minded. He is aware of the possibility of self-deception. Are the spirits real or are they a projection of the people who evoke them? He doesn't profess to know. In future years there are bound to be arguments about the legitimacy of the sources of this poetry, but for me, simply, it all works—as mythology, as history, as a possible interpretation of existence. It works for me as say Dante almost always does and as Blake in the Prophetic Books rather seldom does: the terms are plausible, humane, never arbitrary, and always interesting.

There is indeed a continual consciousness of Dante throughout these works, though wisely no real attempt to imitate him. (It would be an act of desperation to compare them to the *Inferno* and the *Purgatorio*. But many scholars are desperate men and women, and no doubt such detailed comparisons will be made.) But there *is* a great resemblance to Dante, not so much in the fact that the poetry constitutes an ambitious work of other-worldly instruction as in the easy mingling of all the poet's kinds of experience—in particular of personal friends with the famous and historical.

Of other-worldly instruction, there is considerably more in *Mirabell* than there was in 'Ephraim', which in retrospect takes on some of the characteristics of a prologue. Much of *Mirabell* consists of the story of the Fallen Angels, of whom Mirabell is one. They are a race of enormous bats who by their science once raised a 'crust world' into the stratosphere, anchored to the earth at fourteen points by radiated signals. Their sin, the reason that their world breaks apart, was—in both literal and metaphorical terms—that of abandoning earth.

THE 14 POINTS OF CONTACT HELD OUR SKIN IN PLACE   THEY STRAIND
& BROKE & OUR VAST SKEIN OF SMOOTH PLAINS & LATTICE CITIES
(TO OUR EYES FAIR & NATURAL) SHIVERD   BROKE INTO FLAME

(I should point out that spirits speak in upper case.) Much later, in the era of man, the angels are set to work by 'God Biology' to improve and refine souls as they go from body to body, the ultimate aim being to bring about an earthly paradise. The discussion of all this is carried on in a 'seminar' consisting of Merrill, David Jackson, the dead Auden, the dead Maria, and Mirabell.

This book is much more of a straightforward and connected *story* than 'Ephraim'. Merrill feels time pressing in on him, he

> cannot spare those twenty
> Years in a cool dark place that *Ephraim* took
> In order to be palatable wine.

It is plainer, but it is also easier and racier. The exposition of idea, fact, and myth is given narrative pace by a growing 'worldliness' and humanity that Mirabell assumes in contact with the living and dead humans. His style becomes more circumstantial and more metaphorical as the book progresses.

I do not mean to imply that *Mirabell* is all written in one measure or that it is all narrative without variation. The bat-angels speak in prose-like syllabics, the others in metre. Lyrics are embodied in the story. There is also room for flashbacks, asides from the dead Auden on the art of poetry, and incidents that have only indirect bearing on the incidents at the ouija board. The style varies from the simplicity of a phrase like 'the cool, smalltown dawn' to the complexity of this reference to Noah (Mirabell has explained that the Ark carried the dust saved from the Fall—'its particles were/ formulas, atomic structures, communicants of life'):

THAT WAS GOD B'S METHOD & WE, APPROACHING U HANDS CUPPD
WITH LESSONS, HELPD U TO CONSTRUCT A METHOD OF YR OWN.
2 BY 2 WE HAVE ENTERD YR MINDS & NOW YEARS LATER
THE COMMUNICATION IS AFLOAT OVER A DROWND WORLD.

The density of metaphorical life in such a passage gives some indication of the scope, the inclusiveness, the richness of Merrill's heroic enterprise. Fact is seen as metaphor, metaphor as fact; there is a constant movement between the two, making of *Mirabell* a myth even more complex and exciting than 'Ephraim'. Keats spoke of the long poem (as opposed to the short) as somewhere he 'could turn round in', and in *Mirabell* Merrill does indeed turn round and stretch and show us his powers—at their full, I think, for the first time. Elegance has become an extended and graceful strength, and dramatic talent is displayed that never had such a chance before in shorter forms. There are certainly criticisms that can be made— some of them are made by a friend and neighbour, Robert Morse, *in* the poem—but they seem to me small compared with the size of the achievement.

The first person is at last dealt with adequately. It is never suppressed into anonymity, it is never falsified by rhetoric. One of the triumphs, and it is no minor one, of these two long poems, is in Merrill's portrayal of the domestic situation in the middle of which it all takes place. It is also, not incidentally, the most convincing description I know of a gay marriage. Much of what makes any marriage successful is the ability to take the importance of one's partner for granted, to *depend* on the other's love without being in a state of continuous erotic or passional tension. Merrill's indication of these abilities is the firmer for being indirect. The men's life together is presented to us in detail which is almost casual: we see them choosing wallpaper, keeping house, travelling, entertaining, and above all sitting at the ouija board. It is not a minor triumph and it is not an incidental one because, after all, it is the two of them in their closeness who have evoked the whole spirit world of 'Ephraim' and *Mirabell*, or perhaps even created it.

II

AUTOBIOGRAPHY

WRITING A POEM

A few years ago[1] I found myself preoccupied by certain related concepts I wanted to write about. They arose from matters real and imaginary so closely tangled with my life that it was impossible, for the time being, to isolate them as a poem. They were a familiar enough association of ideas, it's true—trust, openness, acceptance, innocence—but I felt them all the more vividly and personally the more signally I failed to get them into poems. Well, I knew by now that the thing to do was not to strain, I'd just have to go on living with the values, watering them, hardening them, getting them bushy with the detail of experience, until their flowering presented itself to me as a given fact. In what sense might you say that innocence can be repossessed, I wondered, and started on yet another sterile poem playing with the figure of a house being repossessed—and if there is one thing innocence is clearly not, it is a house. So at length I put the literary expression out of my mind and either wrote of other things or just let myself go fallow for a while, I forget which.

Then one day I was walking on a hill going down to the Pacific, which it met at a narrow, partly-sheltered beach. I came to the beach from some bushes and was confronted by a naked family—father, mother and small son. The son rushed up to me very excited, shouting 'hi there, hi there' in his shrill voice, and rushed away without waiting for an answer. I walked off and felt happy about the comeliness of the scene: it had, too, a kind of decorum that made my mind return to it several times in the next few hours. I mentioned it to some friends that evening and to others the next

[1] First published in 1973. [Ed.]

day, and the day after that I realized that I wanted to write a poem about the naked family. I didn't know any more than that I wanted to preserve them on paper in the best way I knew, as a kind of supersnapshot, getting my feeling for them into my description of them. It wasn't till the poem was finished that I realized I had among other things found an embodiment for my haunting cluster of concepts, though I hadn't known it at the time.

Looked at one way, idea preceded its embodiment; looked at another, particulars preceded induction. Neither process excludes the other here, because the process of writing a poem is something more comprehensive than either, and I think—in all seriousness and not as a mere playful metaphor—it is also connected with the processes of magic. It is a reaching out into the unexplained areas of the mind, in which the air is too thickly primitive or too fine for us to live continually. From that reaching I bring back loot, and don't always know at first what that loot is, except that I hope it is of value as an understanding or as a talisman, or more likely as a combination of the two, of both rational power and irrational.

When I saw the naked family I didn't know why they satisfied me so much, why I had that strange sense of what I have called decorum. Certainly their appearance was more than a pat embodiment of innocence and its repossession, though as I have said I have come to realize that they were that too. But I did know that I had certain clear and strong feelings about them that I wanted to preserve, if possible by preserving the experience that elicited them. When I came to write the poem, it was all-important that I should be true to those feelings—even, paradoxically, at the risk of distorting the experience. And so for me the act of writing is an exploration, a reaching out, an act of trusting search for the correct incantation that will return me certain feelings whenever I want them. And of course I have never completely succeeded in finding the correct incantations.

MY SUBURBAN MUSE

For most of my adolescence I lived in Hampstead, in the north-west of London. But during the Blitz I was evacuated to a school in the country, where an enlightened English teacher taught from *The Poet's Tongue* (edited by W. H. Auden and John Garrett). It was a remarkable anthology to encounter in 1941, very different from the *Dragon Book of Verse*, which you got in other schools, and which was all Lord Macaulay and the patriotic speeches from *Henry V*. In the introduction to *The Poet's Tongue* poetry was defined as 'memorable speech', still the only workable definition I've come across: and the anthology itself emphasized the range and liveliness of poetry, by including mnemonics, popular songs, mummers' plays, nonsense poetry, songs by Blake, medieval fragments, and at one point two haunting lines from an Elegy of Donne's printed by themselves, as if they were a whole poem:

> Nurse oh My love is slain, I saw him go
> Oer the white alps alone.

Yet though I enjoyed the book I evidently had a more conventional idea of the poetry I wanted to write. Returning to Hampstead at thirteen I read some Greek myths and wrote a poem about a peony, which started:

> O peony you smell
> Like the heavenly nectar Hebe spilt
> On luxurious Olympus.

And about this time I fell for Keats—fell for him as you do for the first poet who really means something to you. I read him all and liked him all, without discrimination, having certain vague yearnings which his poetry answered very satisfactorily. 'I stood tiptoe upon a little hill'—why, it could be Hampstead Heath. In fact, it must have been, because Keats had lived in Hampstead, hadn't he? I doubt if it struck me that Keats's Hampstead had been a village surrounded by real countryside, whereas my Hampstead, though made quiet and almost rural by petrol rationing, was still a part of London—and London at war. If there were cuckoos in the big garden across the road for the last two summers of the war, there were also long convoys of army lorries coiling down Frognal, the houses designed by Freud's son were requisitioned for troops, GIs drank in the William IV and the Flask, and the public library was hit by a V2.

But I found all this easy enough to forget when I was on the Heath. I am still easily moved by the enclosed greenery of parks— as if its being seen by so many humans had brushed off on to it certain slightly human qualities, ranging from the poignant to the sinister. Anyway, for me Hampstead Heath became poeticized by Keats. I particularly liked the view from Judge's Walk; you could gaze from the hill into a distance as brilliantly hazy as it is in Turner's *Crossing the Brook*, which was one of my favourite pictures. I disregarded that what the haze covered was actually only the London suburb of Golders Green. What I encouraged in my poetry, indeed, was less the sharp-eyed exactness of Keats than an air of vague and nebulous beauty that concealed the actual world very nicely. I was prepared to write about a hazy distance of spire and rooftop, but not Golders Green.

I remember I wrote a poem about Eel Pie Island, at Richmond, a compact and pretty place with banks held in by mossy boards, and covered by trees which bulged out romantically over the Thames. But the island I wrote about only took this as its starting point: in the poem it rapidly filled up with ivy-festooned statues of Greek gods and goddesses.

I enjoyed Marlowe and Beddoes and then, when I was seventeen, Meredith. I carried a small red book of Meredith's poetry in my pocket for several months, and read from it so often that I knew some of it by heart. My favourite was 'Love in the Valley', which began:

> Under yonder beechtree, single in the greensward,
> Couched with her arms beneath her golden head,
> Knees and tresses folded to slip and ripple idly,

My young love lies sleeping in the shade.
Had I the heart to slide an arm beneath her,
Press her parting lips as her waist I gather slow,
Waking in amazement she could not but embrace me :
Then would she hold me and never let me go?

I can certainly see the attraction of that metre, but I must say the language is quite a step down from Keats. However, it corresponded to what I now wanted in poetry, and seemed to me positively reckless in its sexiness. One evening in the tube, about this time, I noticed that a rather pretty girl was looking at me, and our eyes met. She was probably merely observing the state of my acne, and of course I never saw her again, but that was all to the good, since I could now imagine her whatever I wanted. The instant, looked back upon, became marked as a memorable lost opportunity. My walks on the Heath became longer and more melancholy. I wrote a poem beginning :

We lay upon a furzy, fire-dry bank
Where green was withered by our passion's flame,
And as there came an ecstasy we drank
Searing salt kisses that quenched not when they came,
Searing salt kisses that quenched not when they came.

I don't remember how it went on (was there anything, indeed, left to add?), but I must have liked that stanza a good deal to be able to write it out from memory twenty-six years later. I was particularly proud of the repeated last line.

I am not trying to sneer at my seventeen-year-old self. Like most people at that age, I had a lot of deep feeling hanging around and didn't quite know what to connect it with. But at least I was trying to do something about it, to assign it some kind of meaning, attach it to something outside of me, even if I wasn't doing it very well. And the poetry I was writing strikes me as constituting a beginning that was perfectly legitimate, and in itself perfectly valueless, like most literary beginnings. I say legitimate, in that it seemed to involve a commitment to writing, and so if I was lucky it might lead somewhere, even though it was all based on illusion and fantasy.

What trite adolescent dreams of being loved by a demonic hero are behind *Wuthering Heights*, what visions of being a dashing young soldier annihilating enemies in battle and breaking hearts in the drawing room are behind Stendhal's novels? Fantasy must always precede fictions, and fictions are as necessary as reality to literature. Love poetry started as the fantasies of troubadours, who by definition had to love at a distance. You can't get the girl you want, so you create a fantasy about her so complete that it can give you some temporary satisfaction. Later I had for a while a theory of poetry as 'loot', a prize grabbed from the outside world and taken permanently into the poet's possession. But of course it isn't taken, it continues out there in the world living its own independent existence, stepping from the tube-train at a later stop, and coolly unaware of all the furore it is causing.

My poems, then, were intensely felt and intensely derivative. At least the intensity was there. What I had to learn was to free myself from too limited a notion of the poetic. I might have had it from *The Poet's Tongue*, that all experience, including Golders Green and acne, is suitable to poetry. But I had to find that out for myself when I was ready. And I would not be ready till I was in my twenties.

CAMBRIDGE IN
THE FIFTIES

I almost didn't go to Cambridge. My headmaster thought I should, and I thought I should, but my father wasn't sure. I wasn't bright enough to get a college scholarship and my father wasn't poor enough for me to apply for a state scholarship. So while I did National Service there was the possibility that I might not actually get there: it was in any case dreadfully distant, an escape from the drudgery of the army into the bright and tranquil life of the mind. I wrote a poem addressed to Cambridge. 'Shall I ever rest on your learned lawns?' I enquired. That was my image of it, a lot of serene young men sitting around on the Backs reading serious books.

So when, during a first roll-call of freshmen in Great Hall at Trinity, a student answered his name with 'Here, Sergeant', and I joined the general titter, it was from relief. We were here at last in Cambridge, actually on the site of learned lawns. We had entered the tradition.

I certainly didn't perceive the snobbery involved. I would have warmly denied it indeed, because my expectation of the place was largely based on the picture given of it in E. M. Forster's *The Longest Journey*. I expected a lot of Ansells and Rickeys, and exciting talks about ideas.

And Cambridge itself collaborated with my expectations. The Master of the college, G. M. Trevelyan, who was by then a very small bent old man, had all the new boys to tea early in that first term, and told us sweetly and learnedly about the buildings and history that we were now the latest instalment of. He showed us an Elizabethan ceiling with great pendulous decorations like stalactites which had been discovered in this century above a false ceiling of a later date, put up when Tudor things had become unfashionable. And he described how one Master, Bentley, had locked all the Fellows in a room until they gave in to his requirements for palatial alterations to his Lodge.

Meanwhile for us there were bedmakers to bring up our shaving water, there were meals in the big shadowy Hall, there was the crisp beauty of the buildings—Neville's Court for perfection, Great Court for show, and Whewell's Court for living in. And even Whewell's Court, where I was for all three years, was a fine example of heavy Victorian Gothic.

One of my contemporaries arrived at Cambridge with a broad Yorkshire accent. But this was 1950, and he made it his business to reform it, so that by the end of the year he was talking through his teeth as affectedly as any of the young gents at the Pitt Club. I wonder if he has since changed it back again.

I was reading English, and shared supervisions with a wonderful Manxman called Seth Caine. We were studying *Piers Plowman* when we found that as members of Trinity all we had to do was ask the librarian and he would show us the fifteenth-century manuscripts in the Wren Library. So we went. He was kind to us and perhaps slightly amused, since we had come not so much to satisfy scholarly curiosity as to test our power.

But historic elegance, detached enlightenment and the life of the mind just about summed up my first year at Cambridge. I read Chaucer and discovered Donne. My supervisor, Helena Shire, worked me hard, and I liked her very much. I tried to smoke a pipe, but kept on coming across a residue of bitter juices from former attempts which was most unpleasant. This was in my first term, when I also toyed with the idea of buying a blazer, and wrote a series of poems about dejected old men walking through dead leaves. Then I became a pacifist. Then I read aloud from left-wing poetry of the thirties at meetings of CUSC, the socialist club, with John Mander, an Etonian Marxist two or three years younger than I, who was writing poetry that seems good to me even today. I couldn't help noticing that his poetry had a vigour somewhat lacking in mine. And as I got toward the end of the academic year I couldn't help feeling, also, that perhaps rather more might have happened to me than the life of the mind. It certainly did seem that there could be parties a bit more exciting than CUSC meetings: one saw dashing undergraduates hurrying *somewhere*, gowns flapping in the wind, and it was evidently toward parties one wasn't asked to. The truth was, I had the desire to be a social climber, but not the talent. I couldn't even find the bottom rung of the ladder, if there was one.

But just at the end of my first year, something did happen. I had a poem published in an anti-war issue of an undergraduate magazine, *Cambridge Today*. The poem was written after seeing the Lewis Milestone film *A Walk in the Sun*, and was predictably Audenesque in idiom. But people reacted to it, another magazine's editor mentioned it in print, and I felt very encouraged. I tore up the poems about the old men and decided to work hard at writing poetry all summer.

The summer vacation was in fact as important as the whole of the preceding year. I read the whole of Shakespeare, and doing that, Helena Shire later remarked, adds a cubit to anybody's stature. And one day, hitch-hiking along a long narrow dusty road in France, I experienced a revelation of physical and spiritual freedom that I still refer to in my thoughts as the Revelation. It was like the elimination of some enormous but undefined problem that had been across my way and prevented me from moving forward. But now I suddenly found I had the energy for almost anything. And wherever I was, working in a farm camp, hitch-hiking through France, and later studying my books at my aunt's in Kent, I pushed myself through an apprenticeship in poetry. I was greatly influenced by Auden still—in one poem I even addressed Picasso as 'Sir', imitating Auden's Hopkinsey invocation to God, 'Sir, no man's enemy . . .' And Donne gave me the licence both to be obscure and to find material in the contradictions of one's own emotions. But I wrote steadily, averaging about a poem a week, and was to continue doing so without stop for at least another year and a half.

Right from the start the second year was busier than the first. Apparently that single, derivative poem had had the authority to get me taken seriously by the other poets. That autumn a group of us would get together every week to discuss each other's work— Norman Buller and Harold Silver, I think, and maybe I knew John Coleman that early, and John Mander, who was still a communist but was soon to become an Anglo-Catholic and amaze me with talk of heresies, a word I had seen in print but had never heard spoken before. They were good practical little meetings, as I remember, in which we tried to suppress our own vanities and be of help to each other.

One windy autumn night I was walking along Jesus Lane from one of these meetings. Coming to the corner of Sidney Street, I could see my own window above. Friends would shout up to me from this street corner, to save themselves climbing two flights of stairs to find if I was in. I noticed that I had left my light on and found myself imagining that I had called my name aloud and could now see my own head stick out of the window above. There were times when anything seemed possible.

Meanwhile I was going to all of F. R. Leavis's lectures, though it was earlier, at the end of the previous year, that I had discovered him. He attracted me as few other teachers at Cambridge did: it is true that his lectures were prepared monologues like everybody else's, but they seemed to have the improvisatory character of discussions. And he was frank about his passion for literature—it was for him important because of its bearing upon experience, no less. If this passion sometimes made him argumentative or undignified, so much the worse for those he argued with, it all helped to validate his approach. I could see it all, this commitment to literature, as neither pastime nor occasion for scholarship, it was after all the reason I had wanted to read English in the first place. And his discriminations and enthusiasms helped teach me to write, better than any creative-writing class could have. His insistence on the realized, being the life of poetry, was exactly what I needed. His perceptions about language and verse movement in discussing the first line of 'Burnt Norton', of Wordsworth's 'Surprised by joy', of 'If it were done when 'tis done', for example—by going directly to the texture of poetry, by showing how the reader's halting and attentive voice is an equivalent to the poet's act of exploration, by risking close scrutiny that entered into the terms of creation—brought me right to the hearth of my own activity. I was the victim of large, vague, diffused emotions. Seeing them as too diffused I had tried to turn my back on them, and had written my poems about old men who possessed only minimal emotions. But Leavis's lectures helped me to deal directly with my own, by reducing their diffusion, by concentrating them.

Yet there was an orthodoxy. I had to learn without becoming a disciple, for disciples have a tendency to turn observation into doctrine. But I was not after all one of Leavis's students and indeed met him only once personally, and then it was in my third year. So I learnt what I could and then ran off with it. Which is not to say that I don't look back upon his lectures with gratitude and love.

I was to have several close friends who read English at Leavis's college, Downing, but they were all in some way a bit alienated from the master himself. It was in fact about this time, at the beginning of my second year, that I met a brilliant young freshman from Downing, a Scot named Karl Miller. Argumentative, inquisitive, imaginative, he seemed to have no preconceived ideas of what he might find at Cambridge and he wasn't going to accept anybody else's. His very abrasiveness was part of his charm. And he charmed me off my feet, as he did everybody whom he didn't irritate, and I stuck by his side, all admiration, for the next year.

When I wrote a new poem I would give it to him for criticism, and he would pin it to the wall above his desk for several days before he told me what he thought of it. He helped me in other and greater ways. He matured my mind amazingly, and I learned from his habit of questioning, of questioning everything. There was always something rather childish about the way I submitted to the enthusiasms of others. If I learned to argue with them a little, it was from him.

I no longer wanted to be a social climber. The people I knew now were much too exciting for me to want to go beyond them. Another friend from Downing was John Coleman, a poet and reviewer. He was so wise and worldly that I was once heard to say, 'Five minutes with John Coleman and all my problems are solved.' His affectionately witty manner struck me as the last word in sophistication. I wrote a poem to him beginning 'You understand both Adolphe and Fabrice'. And he did too, though he was not to be without his problems. Some time after I first knew him he was walking one evening with a girl on a Cambridge street, neither of them in the black gowns students were then supposed to wear after dark. Proctors appeared to question them; they answered with assumed voices and farcical accents, for which they were sent down from Cambridge.

Meanwhile, independently of my friends, I was trying to develop certain thoughts. They amounted to a rather crude theory of what I called 'pose', based partly on the dramatics of John Donne, somewhat perhaps on Yeats's theory of masks, and most strongly on the behaviour of Stendhal's heroes. I was to find support for it from other sources, notably from some of Shakespeare's characters, like the Bastard in *King John* and Coriolanus, and later from Sartre. It was, as you can see, literary in character, but its principal source was the Revelation on the road in France, with its intimations of unbounded energy. The theory of pose was this: everyone plays a part, whether he knows it or not, so he might as well deliberately design a part, or a series of parts, for himself. Only a psychopath or a very good actor is in danger of *becoming* his part, however, so one who is neither is left in an interesting place somewhere in between the starting point—the bare undefined and undirected self, if he ever existed—and the chosen part. This is a place rich in tensions between the achieved and the unachieved. I thought of Julien Sorel with Madame Rénal, the counterpoint a man's vulnerable emotions made upon his seduction timed by the clock.

To tell the truth, I don't remember doing much about my theory in the actual living of my life, but viewing myself as an actor trying to play a part provided rich material for poetry. It also provided opportunities for falling flat on my face once I forgot the more ridiculous possibilities implicit in the whole theory. One of the poems I wrote during this year was called 'A Village Edmund', referring to Edmund in *King Lear*. It concluded thus:

> When it was over he pulled his trousers on.
> 'Demon lovers must go,' he coldly said,
> And she stared at the pale intolerable moon.

Towards the end of my second year I met Tony White, another student from Downing. I had been aware of him for a long time, as many others had, for he was a rising local actor. He had played, or shortly was to play, Aufidius, Astrov, Gaveston, Mark Antony (in *Julius Caesar*), Petruchio, Romeo, and Cyrano, among other parts, as romantic-existentialist characters. The similarity between the parts is not great, perhaps it was an error that he made it so, but the vigour of the interpretations amounted to a unifying style. If his Aufidius was slightly more sensitive than one would have expected, one might almost say more alienated, then his Romeo was also more of a tough than he is usually seen to be. For his interpretation of Romeo, indeed, Tony took as a guiding hint the scene with the apothecary near the end—a certain callousness qualifies the romantic obsession, but maybe also makes his absorption in it possible. But in all the parts, as he played them, there was a kind of athletic defiance of the gods.

We first met at a party, where we joyfully discussed Stendhal for about two hours. We were later to find many other shared enthusiasms. But, well as I came to know him at Cambridge, I think I took him at face value at this time, and it was easy to do so, his surface was so finished, so lively and delightful in itself. He was a man of courtesy, and I mean courtesy not merely in a social sense. It was a giving of himself, in all his strength and sweetness, to others, whom he admired more than he could ever admire himself. His courtesy was a direct result of the deep unease in him, a defiance of it. And ultimately he wasn't able to keep up the kind of self-regard which would have been necessary for him to continue as an actor.

Anyway, from the time I met him till his death as the result of a football accident at the age of forty-five, he was one of the most important people in my life. If I was not yet to learn the real vulnerabilities in him for a while (and they were vulnerabilities that in others would have seemed like strengths), we were still becoming tied to each other by mutual enthusiasm. He seemed to articulate in a bolder way than I ever could the kind of personal freedom that I had glimpsed on the road in France : he was a model as well as a friend. He helped me to shape my thoughts. It was he who first got me to read Sartre's plays and Camus's novels. (They were not yet taught in universities.) He introduced me to his friends who had already left Cambridge. We formed projects together, we studied books together, we even found, to our amusement, that we both affected the same check shirts, which we had bought on Charing Cross Road, making us look, we hoped, more like Canadian loggers than Cambridge undergraduates.

I have a card from him which must date from a bit later, the beginning of 1954 :

All my best wishes for
panache, logique, espagnolisme,
l'imprévu, singularité and
MAGNANIMITY
in the New Year
from one Étranger
to another

He was certainly fully aware of the comic implications of our home-made philosophy, the mélange of Rostand, Stendhal, Shakespeare, and Camus.

Cambridge had not before seemed so rich in its fulfilment of possibilities. I had a lot of exciting friends, I was doing well in my exams, and there was the summer. The winter of Cambridge is so bleak, so unremitting, that the early summer always seems like a gift; it is even greater than anything one could possibly have *earned* by suffering through the other seasons. I have memories of charming idylls such as every undergraduate has always had: of sitting on the Backs in early evening listening to the long calls of the birds as they went to their nests, of bicycling out past the fields to supervisions at Conduit Head Road and once of clearing the orchard there with a billhook, and of a time very close before exams when some of us took off the afternoon and punted down to Grantchester and back, Karl Miller improvising ballads about the people in the boat, particularly about Geoffrey Strickland, in stanzas that started 'Now old Sir Geoffrey . . .'.

And a play was put on, *The Taming of the Shrew*. Toby Robertson directed it, his sister Toppit played Katherine, Tony White played Petruchio, and other friends like Sasha Moorsom were in it. I was persuaded to play First Servant, and as Second Servant almost never turned up to rehearsals I got his lines too. It was played during May Week, three nights in Trinity Fellows' Garden and three nights in King's Fellows' Garden. In the last scene as night came on, the servants held up flaming torches. It was Cambridge at its sweetest—Shakespeare, the moonlit summer night, the park-like private gardens of wealthy colleges, friends I hoped would be friends for life—different kinds of happiness rolled into one.

Yet there was no fixed Cambridge. There was instead a number of beautifully kept-up old buildings and a core of teachers and retainers. This was a background against which a lot of intelligent young people improvised their fantasies of what 'Cambridge' might be. The fantasies could be sporty or scholarly, they might be about artistic community or gilded youth, but they were all essentially derivative, and it was the derivativeness that provided continuity. My Forsterian fantasy had been brought up to date but also enriched and extended by the fantasies of my friends. And apparently, whether we were conscious of it or not, our fantasies—which we speedily fulfilled—had to do with success.

I conclude this, not because I can remember making my bid for local fame, but because in my third year I got it and people seldom become successful without wanting to be. There was always a niche for the Cambridge Poet (as for the Cambridge Politician, the Cambridge Editor, and the Cambridge Actor), and I was indeed happy to occupy it now that John Mander had given up writing. I edited an anthology of student poetry. I was now president of the English Club, with Karl doing the hard work, as secretary. As such, I gave embarrassed introductions to Angus Wilson, Henry Green, Dylan Thomas (sober and punctual), W. W. Robson, Kathleen Raine, Bonamy Dobrée, William Empson, and other writers who came to speak to us. And Mark Boxer (the cartoonist Marc) asked me to help with the magazine *Granta*, of which he was editor, but that worked out only for a short time, even though I continued to publish in it.

Looking back on that time, I can see it all as a bit incestuous: we promoted each other consistently. For example, the university newspaper *Varsity* featured a profile of a local celebrity each week, and it seems to me that we all wrote each other's profiles, thus creating and perpetuating each other's celebrity.

I now went to as many chic parties as I wanted to, but I wanted to less and less. I had a sense of the whole thing stiffening, there was less of that fine feeling of flexibility that there had been the year before.

I do remember one remarkable party, or rather Karl told me about it because I passed out from drinking about a half-gallon of sherry. It took place at Newnham, and a don had to be specially brought from her bed, in her nightdress and dressing-gown, to open a side gate, normally locked, so that I could be carried more easily to a waiting taxi. She stood there in pained silence, waiting to give permission for the closing of the gate, and it seems that as I was being hauled past her my unconscious body gave a terrific fart, as if adding the sin of ingratitude to that of gluttony. I do not remember this personally, but I have Karl's word for it.

There was later a memorable escapade. About six of us, three boys and three girls, decided to go to Paris for a week. So after my yearly Christmas job with the post office, I went over to stay with John Coleman, who was now teaching in a school near there. The place he had borrowed from a gym teacher was far too small, so we all moved to a cheap hotel on the Rue Jacob, sleeping in two rooms. Paris was iron-cold, and we had a wonderful time, though I can't remember the order in which things happened very well. The group kept separating, reforming, and separating again. We ate horsemeat steaks and black sausage on the Boulevard St-Germain. Tony had met a French girl on the boat and she asked him and me round to dinner with her family, where the father kept putting down Shakespeare as a barbarian who couldn't observe the unities. We saw *Phèdre* at the Comédie Française, done in much the same style as in the seventeenth century. One of us, John Holmstrom, bought some books by Genet, which he intended to smuggle back into England, these being banned books. And I found myself somehow spending the end of New Year's Eve alone in someone else's room at the top of a smelly tenement. I opened the windows before I went to sleep and drunkenly watched the big damp snowflakes as they fell through the patch of light. A couple of days later Tony and Bronwyn O'Connor and I returned across the Channel together, sitting on the deck singing music-hall songs so that we wouldn't think about being sick.

Then we went back for our last two terms at Cambridge. The best thing about being an undergraduate at Oxford or Cambridge was that you were trusted to do the work more or less in your own time and to feed on what authors you would. I now went to almost no lectures in English, but to some in the French and History Faculties. And it must have been around this time that I realized I was getting more education from my contemporaries than from my teachers. Moreover I don't think I met any teachers at Cambridge in the whole of my first two years, apart from my supervisors. In my third year I did meet a few, but largely because I went to the right parties.

Meanwhile Mark Boxer was sent down for 'blasphemy', because *Granta* published a poem uncomplimentary to God. Its sophistication is sufficiently indicated by the lines, 'You drunken gluttonous seedy God,/You son of a bitch, you snotty old sod.' It is hard to believe that such a poem should have caused a scandal, and in fact the scandal was caused only for the Proctors. But it was the Proctors who had the power to send Mark down and to ban *Granta* for a year. However, some undergraduates, graduates, and dons revived the magazine under the name of *Gadfly*, of which the format and contributors were identical. It even contained drawings by Mark.

One morning I read in the *News Chronicle* of Dylan Thomas's death. Karl had taught me to love his poetry. I went round to Karl's room and, not finding him there, left a solemn little note on his mantelpiece: 'This is a black day for English poetry', so that he should know I was feeling the proper grief.

And from around this time I find an issue of a mimeographed periodical called *Broadsheet*, in which a reviewer ends his piece with these words: 'Since writing this article I have met E. J. Hughes, of Pembroke, who is trying to bring writers of poetry in Cambridge together at the Anchor, where the landlord has set aside a room for the display of poetry.' E. J. Hughes of Pembroke was very retiring. I am not sure if I even knew him to speak to while I was at Cambridge, though I did know what he looked like. We did not become friends until years later, after he had, as Ted Hughes, published his first book.

As the year went on, I withdrew more and more from the 'Cambridge' I had helped create. I had fallen in love, but that is another story. In any case I felt a pull away from the place.

In the summer I hung on after the term was over, deciding for indefinite reasons to take my degree in person, in wing collar, bow tie, and rented suit. Most of my friends did it by proxy and it was already the tourist season, the Backs and the river covered by straying families with cameras and sandwiches. But I was still a part of it for a few more days before I joined the families as one who had no place here.

What I was to realize more clearly after I had gone down was that, for all who go there, whether rich or poor (or, most likely, middle class), Cambridge is a place of privilege, and things are usually made easier for those who have been there. My first books were reviewed more kindly than they deserved largely, I think, because London expected good poets to emerge from Oxford and Cambridge and here I was, somebody new with all the fashionable influences and coming from Cambridge. I am not implying that those who treated me so well when I started publishing were consciously playing favourites, but I know that they were mostly from Oxford and

Cambridge themselves and that *I got a hearing* more readily than if I had just graduated from the University of Hull.

Many of my contemporaries went on to become well known—as directors of plays, actors, editors of magazines, historians, reviewers, novelists, dramatists. London received them warmly, and being talented they flourished in the warmth. Only Tony White, among my close friends, became an exception: he joined the Old Vic company, and had got so far after a few years as to play Cassio in *Othello* when he dropped it all, for a life of odd jobs and translating, barely making ends meet as a handyman, plumber, house painter, or translator of some lengthy anthropological work from French into English. He dropped out, coolly and deliberately, from the life of applause, having come to see how the need for it complicates one's existence quite unnecessarily.

So I am grateful to Cambridge for many things. It enriched my life enormously, it gave me the security and advantages that everybody ought to have, but it also brought me up against someone who could eventually teach me that the real business was elsewhere completely.

MY LIFE UP TO NOW

One day my father, who was a journalist, came home with a dummy newspaper for me. That is, it said *Daily Express* at the top, it was divided into columns, and it even had a space for the Stop Press, or late news. But otherwise it was blank, and there were no headlines or stories or pictures. So I filled it all in with a pencil. I couldn't write words, but I got a lot of satisfaction from drawing pictures and then surrounding them with line after line of scribble. And this is the first creative act I can remember.

My father was the son of a merchant seaman whose family had emigrated from north-east Scotland to Kent some time in the nineteenth century. He was devoted to his job, working for the Beaverbrook press for many years, but eventually, in the early fifties, becoming editor of the *Daily Sketch*, the circulation of which he raised to over a million. He was a man full of charm who made friends easily; I remember in my childhood how exciting the house was on his days off, crowded with his colleagues and their wives—every weekend seemed like a party. But he and my mother were divorced when I was eight or nine, and I never found myself close to him. Neither of us ever invited each other into any intimacy: from my mid-teens onward we were jealous and suspicious of each other, content merely to do our duty and no more.

I was close to my mother and, while I never heard much about my father's family, the history of my mother's formed a kind of basic mythology for me. The Thomsons were Baptists from a village called Echt near Aberdeen. Toward the end of the last century the eldest son went down to Kent to try his luck as the bailiff of a farm. His luck was so good that he sent for his mother and all his brothers and sisters, like Joseph in Egypt sending home for the rest of his family—the parallel cannot have failed to strike the Bible-minded Thomsons—and by the start of this century each of the brothers was established as a tenant farmer in the villages between Maidstone and Rochester, my grandfather Alexander's farm being in Snodland.

They and their families were characteristic country Nonconformists of the time, Baptists on the way to becoming Methodists. They venerated education and despised frivolity—of which the idolatry of Catholics was the most pernicious example. They were pacifists, Keir Hardie socialists, and anti-royalists—the last because they considered the Royal Family not only outdated but corrupt. (They still believe that Mary, the Princess Royal, was 'lost in a card game' to her future husband by her brother, George V.) Before World War I, one of my great-uncles went to jail for a weekend for refusing to pay tithes, and briefly became a local hero.

My mother was one of seven children, all girls, and all of a very independent turn of mind. (I am for ever grateful that my brother and I were brought up in no religion at all.) She became a journalist, meeting my father in the office of the *Kent Messenger*, but stopped working before I was born in 1929. When I was about four I got lost in Kensington Gardens; a policeman asked me what my mother was like: I described her as 'a proud woman'. Like her sisters, she was something of a feminist, though the word was not used in those days. At the same time she enjoyed fashion—how her smart clothes and her hennaed hair mortified me when my school friends saw her—but was prepared to give it her own turn. She was once seen at a party wearing an orchid pinned by a brooch in the shape of hammer and sickle. From this distance the combination sounds like a cliché of the thirties, but it wasn't: other women wouldn't have done something so outrageous. I see behind it an impudent and witty proclamation that she wanted to get the best of both worlds, and at the same time I can see the half-rueful self-criticism.

And the house was full of books. When she was pregnant with me she read the whole of Gibbon's *History*. From her I got the complete implicit idea, from as far back as I can remember, of books as not just a commentary on life but a part of its continuing activity.

The first book I read by myself was Louisa Alcott's *Little Men*, and all that stays in my mind from it is the character of Dan, the rebellious boy who is out of place among the pieties of Dr Baer's model school : I have liked the name Dan ever since. As for poetry, probably my earliest models, after nursery rhymes, were the poems in Arthur Mee's *Children's Encyclopedia*, by Victorians like Jean Ingelow and Charles Kingsley. The books that meant most to me, however, were prose romances—George Macdonald's and John Masefield's books for children, and all the novels of that sensible and imaginative woman E. Nesbit.

I wrote poems and small stories, but only occasionally, and I suspect that when I did so it was often as much for the approval of adults as for my own satisfaction. But I do remember that when I was eight I once sat down and wrote character sketches of all the boys in my form at school. That was done for myself alone, and the process of rendering them in words interested me, just as much with the boys I disliked or felt indifferent to as with my friends.

I had a happy childhood. Because of changes in my father's job, we moved around the country a lot at first, but finally we settled down in Hampstead, not then nearly as wealthy a place as it now is. It was quiet and rather old-fashioned. I played with my friends on the Heath, fording streams or skirmishing with strange children.

My younger brother Ander (his name was short for Alexander) was a partner in a lot of these games, we being fairly close in age. Early in our lives he and I had been cast in the roles of, respectively, extrovert and introvert, I am sure unfortunately, and so our interests tended to be complementary rather than identical. But we always had a firm friendly relationship, sometimes playing together and as often going our own ways.

At the time of the Blitz we were sent for a year or so to a boarding school in Hampshire. While I was there, my mother asked me to write a 'novel' for her birthday. So during siesta every day I wrote in a notebook until it was full. The result was a story called *The Flirt*, curiously sophisticated for a twelve-year-old. It was written in short chapters and illustrated with pictures cut out of my mother's magazines, chiefly *Vogue*. It was the story of the courtship, marriage, and divorce of an aging Lothario known as the Colonel (based, for his physical characteristics, on the cartoonist David Low's Colonel Blimp, with his bald head and white walrus moustache). In an almost wholly female society he is constantly patronized and jeered at, yet it is he who survives at the end, with a new girl on his arm. (Most of the other characters die, the heroine out of simple poverty as the result of having become an unsuccessful prostitute.) One reason for the preponderance of women may be that the pictures from *Vogue* were unlikely to be of men, but because I had far more female relatives than male I knew what such a society was like. And interestingly enough there is a lot of covert sympathy shown by the author for the Colonel, since he (my father? me?), however spineless, remains jovial, slow-witted, and warm-hearted to the end.

I was reading adult books by this time, devouring H. G. Wells, for example, and perhaps already the early issues of *Penguin New Writing*, but I'd be hard put to say what was behind *The Flirt*. This interesting production had no successor, however, and eventually in my teens I became concerned with grandiloquence, under the influence first of Marlowe and Keats, then of Milton, then of Victorians like Tennyson and Meredith. I wanted by then to *be a writer*: the role was all-important, was in fact a good part of the writing's subject-matter.

Well, I'm glad I got much of that out of my system relatively early. Meanwhile I was back in London, eyeing the well-fed and good-looking G.I.s who were on every street, with an appreciation I didn't completely understand. I was back at University College School, a day-school I attended for about ten years (apart from the break forced by the Blitz). I enjoyed being there: it was not very good academically, I suppose, at least during World War II, but it was a tolerant and easy-going school, and the headmaster, C. S. Walton, was an impressive and exemplary figure for me, who covertly helped me through some early difficulties with my father. After my mother's death when I was fifteen, I lived with family friends in Hampstead during the weekdays of the term and with two of my aunts in Snodland during the weekends and vacations. My aunts had a milk-round on which I sometimes helped out, serving the milk out of pails into covered jugs left outside or inside back doors. Then I did my two years national service in the army. Apart from the first ten weeks of basic training, which were at least exuberantly healthy, the two years were largely a matter of boredom, drudgery, and endurance, as they were for most of the rest of my generation. After that I worked in Paris for six months at a job, something of a low-paid sinecure, that a friend of my father's had got for me, and then I went to Cambridge in 1950.

During the whole of this time, from the beginning of 1945 to

1950, I was trying to write novels and poetry, but the results were imitative and dispiriting. I was still copying, of course, as I had earlier been copying on the dummy newspaper, and the imperfections in the copying could have been the beginning of my own real writing. But something was in the way; there was some kind of material that I wasn't able to face up to. I'm not certain what it was: it wasn't simply that I couldn't yet acknowledge my homosexuality, though that was part of it. It was more that my imagination retreated too easily into the world before my mother's death, a world that in practice excluded most of the twentieth century. I read an enormous number of nineteenth-century novels in my teens. It was the present that I couldn't deal with in my imagination or in fact. The army, surprisingly, had been of some help, by forcing me into what were for me extreme situations with which it was necessary to cope for the sake of survival. But by twenty-one I was strangely immature, a good deal more so than any of my friends.

My first year at Cambridge changed that, and by the end of it my emotional age had just about caught up with my actual age. In the next two years, 1951 to 1953, I wrote almost all the poems that were to be published as my first book, *Fighting Terms*. In 1952, my first poem to be 'published' nationally, 'The Secret Sharer', was broadcast by John Lehmann on his BBC programme *New Soundings*. I was still influenced by dead writers—especially the Elizabethans— but they were writers I could see as *bearing upon* the present, upon my own activities. Donne and Shakespeare spoke living language to me, and it was one I tried to turn to my own uses. Suddenly everything started to feed my imagination. Writing poetry became the act of an existentialist conqueror, excited and aggressive. (Robert Duncan uses the same image for the poet, that of the conqueror, in *Caesar's Gate*, but I wasn't to hear of him for several years.) What virtues this collection possesses, however, are mostly to be found in an awareness of how far I fell short of being such a conqueror. Proust and Stendhal as well as Shakespeare and Donne had taught me to watch for the inconsistencies of the psyche.

The image of the soldier recurs in this book, as it does I suppose throughout my work. First of all he is myself, the national serviceman, the 'clumsy brute in uniform', the soldier who never goes to war, whose role has no function, whose battledress is a joke. Secondly, though, he is a 'real' soldier, both ideal and ambiguous, attractive and repellent: he is a warrior and a killer, or a career man in peace-time, or even a soldier on a quest like Odysseus or Sir Gawain. (I read *Sir Gawain and the Green Knight* at Cambridge, and it took possession of that part of my mind that had wondered at George Macdonald's prose when I was younger and at Browning's 'Childe Roland to the Dark Tower Came' in my teens.) In a poem called 'The Wound', which comes in this book, the speaker is both —at one time Achilles, the real soldier in a real war, and at another time the self who dreamt he was Achilles.

(Perhaps I should here note that when Jerome Rothenberg published *Fighting Terms* in the US in 1958, I had put the whole book through a rigorous revision. Then when Faber and Faber published it in 1962 I *de*revised it somewhat. Several people complained about the alterations in both editions, and I can now see how I was tidying up something I oughtn't to have tampered with. By regularizing things so much, I was taking from whatever quality that first book had, a kind of rhetorical awkwardness. I would now reprint it pretty much as it appeared in the first edition, though continuing to omit two minor catastrophes, one, 'Contemplative and Active', for being dull, and the other, 'A Village Edmund', for being unintentionally comic.)

It was around the time of the original publication of this book, 1954, or perhaps a little earlier, that I first heard of something called the Movement. To my surprise, I also learned that I was a member of it. (Vernon Watkins told me that he had had a similar experience in the early 1940s with the New Apocalypse.) It originated as a half-joke by Anthony Hartley writing in the *Spectator* and then was perpetuated as a kind of journalistic convenience. What poets like Larkin, Davie, Elizabeth Jennings, and I had in common at that time was that we were deliberately eschewing Modernism, and turning back, though not very thoroughgoingly, to traditional resources in structure and method. But this was what most of the other poets of our age (even many Americans) were doing in the early fifties. When an anthology from a rival group called the Mavericks appeared, it was hard to see any essential difference between the kind of poems that they and we were writing. The whole business looks now like a lot of categorizing foolishness.

My poetry was far more influenced by people I met at Cambridge, Karl Miller, John Mander, and John Coleman, and to a much greater extent Tony White, the soul of our generation, who remained throughout his life my best reader and most helpful critic, knowing what I was trying to get at in poems often so bad that it's difficult to see how he divined my intentions. I went to the lectures of F. R. Leavis, then in his prime, whose emphasis on the 'realized' in imagery and on the way in which verse movement is an essential part of the poet's exploration were all-important for me.

Also at Cambridge I met Mike Kitay, an American, who became the leading influence on my life, and thus on my poetry. It is not easy to speak of a relationship so long-lasting, so deep, and so complex, nor of the changes it has gone through, let alone of the effect it has had on my writing. But his was, from the start, the example of the searching worrying improvising intelligence playing upon the emotions which in turn reflect back on the intelligence. It was an example at times as rawly passionate as only Henry James can dare to be.

In my last year at Cambridge, I edited an anthology of under-graduate (and some graduate) poetry of the previous two years. It says something about the literary climate in Cambridge at the time : I was not alone in being influenced by the metaphysical poets of the seventeenth century, for example. The prevailing tone is clever, bookish, and spirited.

After I left Cambridge I spent some months in Rome on a student-ship (though I came back to Cambridge for the following spring and summer to stay in the Central Hotel). In front of a new notebook I wrote :

> A style is built with sedentary toil
> And constant imitation of great masters.

The master I chose to imitate that winter was the author of these lines, Yeats. Little got finished, as a result : Yeats was too hypnotic an influence, and my poetry became awash with his mannerisms. Of the great English poets he is probably the second most disastrous influence after Milton. The skills to be learned are too closely tied in with the mannerisms.

I found that the only way to get to the United States, where I intended to eventually join Mike (who had to go into the air force) was to get a fellowship at some university. An American friend, Donald Hall, wrote suggesting that I should apply for a creative-writing fellowship at Stanford University, where I would work unde Yvor Winters, with whose very name I was unfamiliar. I applied, and was fortunate enough to get it, so in 1954 I set out for America, spending my twenty-fifth birthday in mid-Atlantic and landing in New York during a hurricane. What followed was a beautiful year, during which I wrote most of what was to become my second book. I had a room, for fifteen dollars a month, at the top of an old shingled house on Lincoln Avenue in Palo Alto. The eaves stretched down beside the window where I sat at my desk; I could watch the squirrels leaping about on it as I wrote.

I went several times into San Francisco. It was still something of an open city, with whore-houses flourishing for anybody to see. A straight couple took me to my first gay bar, the Black Cat. It excited me so much that the next night I returned there on my own. And I remember walking along Columbus Avenue on another day, thinking that the ultimate happiness would be for Mike and me to settle in this city. It was foggy and I remember exactly where I thought this, right by a cobbler's that still stands there.

But for most of that year I was some thirty miles away down the Peninsula, and the person I had most to do with was Yvor Winters. It was wonderful luck for me that I should have worked with him at this particular stage of my life, rather than earlier when I would have been more impressionable or later when I would have been less ready to learn. As it was, he acted as a fertilizing agent, and opened the way to many poets I had known little of—most immediately Williams and Stevens, whom he insisted I read without delay. He was a man of great personal warmth with a deeper love for poetry than I have ever met in anybody else. The love was behind his increasingly strict conception of what a poem should and should not be. It would have seemed to him an insult to the poem that it could be used as a gymnasium for the ego. Poetry was an instrument for exploring the truth of things, as far as human beings can explore it, and it can do so with a greater verbal exactitude than prose can manage. Large generalized feelings (as in Whitman) were out, and rhetoric was the beginning of falsification. However, taken as I was with the charm and authority of the man and with the power of his persuasiveness, it already seemed to me that his conception of a poem was too rigid, excluding in practice much of what I could not but consider good poetry, let us say 'Tom o' Bedlam' and 'The force that through the green fuse drives the flower'. The rigidity seemed to be the result of what I can only call an increasing distaste for the particulars of existence.

The Sense of Movement, then, was a much more sophisticated book than my first collection had been, but a much less independent one. There is a lot of Winters in it, a fair amount of Yeats, and a great deal of raw Sartre (strange bedfellows!). It was really a second work of apprenticeship. The poems make much use of the word 'will'. It was a favourite word of Sartre's, and one that Winters appreciated, but they each meant something very different by it, and would have understood but not admitted the other's use of it. What *I* meant by it was, ultimately, a mere Yeatsian wilfulness. I was at my usual game of stealing what could be of use to me.

It is still a very European book in its subject-matter. I was much taken by the American myth of the motorcyclist, then in its infancy, of the wild man part free spirit and part hoodlum, but even that I started to anglicize: when I thought of doing a series of motorcyclist poems I had Marvell's mower poems in my mind as model.

At the end of the year I went, for the second time, to Texas by rail, but this time stopped off for a few days in Los Angeles. It was mid-1955, and Los Angeles was a place of wonder to me: it was already the city of *Rebel Without a Cause*, a movie that had not yet been made. The place was as foreign and exotic to me as ever Venice or Rome had been—the huge lines of palms beside the wide fast streets, the confident shoddiness of Hollywood Boulevard, and the dirty glamour of a leather bar called the Cinema, which was on Santa Monica Boulevard, almost a part of a closed gas station and right across from a vast cemetery.

I had been given an introduction to Christopher Isherwood. He asked me over to the set of a movie for which he had written the script, *Diane*, starring Lana Turner as Diane de Poitiers. He was all warmth and kindness to the rather pushy English boy who had turned up out of the blue, and ended up by asking me to a dinner he had already been invited to, at Gerald Heard's. I had my own ideas about Heard, and argued brashly with him for much of the evening.

I can hardly say that meeting Isherwood was the start of the influence he has had on me, but it strengthened it and made it personal. In his talk, as in his books, he is able to present complexity through the elegance of simplicity, but without ever reducing it *to* mere simplicity. And such a manner was just what I needed to learn from.

I joined Mike in San Antonio, Texas, where I taught for a year. English friends thought it sounded an amusing place to be: we found it distinctly boring, starting with the hot and humid climate. However, the sand storms were of interest to one who had never seen them. Also, I got a motorcycle which I rode for about one month, and it was in San Antonio that I heard Elvis Presley's songs first and that I saw James Dean's films. I wrote only three poems during the whole year.

Then, full of nostalgia for the smell of eucalyptus in the dry sunshine of the San Francisco Peninsula, I dragged Mike back with me to do graduate work at Stanford, where I had got a teaching assistantship. On the way, while he stayed with his parents, I spent a few weeks in New York, beginning a lifelong romance with it. If England is my parent and San Francisco is my lover, then New York is my own dear old whore, all flash and vitality and history.

Back at Stanford, Winters encouraged me to attend his workshops regularly, but I went to them less and less, from something of an instinct for self-preservation. The man was too strong; and for all my gratitude to him I knew I had, if necessary, to write my own bad poetry and explore its implications for myself. And I never did get a PhD. Most of the graduate work began to seem pointless after a while, and I had already decided not to go on with it when I was lucky enough to get an offer to teach English at the University of California at Berkeley, in 1958.

I lived for a couple of years in Oakland, a drab town next to Berkeley, then in 1960 spent several months on leave in Berlin, where I wrote the last poems to be included in my next book. When I returned, it was to San Francisco, across the Bay, and I still live there. San Francisco is a provincial town that goes in and out of fashion, but it is never boring and has much of the feel of the big city without trying to master you as the big city does. It leaves you alone: sitting in my yard, now, I could be a hundred miles away from San Francisco.

In the late fifties and early sixties I wrote a series of omnibus poetry reviews for the *Yale Review*. It is always good to make yourself read poetry with close attention, but I became more and more dissatisfied with the business of making comparatively fast judgements on contemporary poets. Specifically, there were books that I simply changed my mind about later on. For example, when it first came out, I sneered at Williams's final book to *Paterson*, and it wasn't until a few years later that I came to revere it as the great epilogue to a great work. And I am haunted by a remark I made about Howard Nemerov, based on a magnificent but unique poem : a piece of praise so high that it is still reprinted on his dust-jackets.

I stopped regular reviewing because I felt more and more that I had to live with a book for some time before I could really find out its value for me. And I was less ready to say unkind things about those who were practising the same art as I was, however differently. I have certainly done reviews and essays since 1964, but only about poets I liked.

In 1961 I published *My Sad Captains*, the name of the title poem having been suggested by Mike. The collection is divided into two parts. The first is the culmination of my old style—metrical and rational but maybe starting to get a little more humane. The second half consists of a taking up of that humane impulse in a series of poems in syllabics. Writing in a new form almost necessarily invited new subject-matter, and in such a poem as 'Adolescence' I was writing a completely different kind of poem from any I had done before. But after this book I couldn't go much further with syllabics, even though I did write other poems in the form during the next few years. It was really, it turned out, a way of teaching myself about unpatterned rhythms—that is, about free verse. But I have not abandoned metre, and in trying to write in both free verse and metre I think I am different from a lot of my contemporaries. Poets who started writing in the early fifties began with metre and rhyme, but most of them—especially the Americans —who switched to free verse at the end of the decade rounded on their earlier work with all the savagery of the freshly converted. I haven't done so : there are things I can do in the one form that I can't do in the other, and I wouldn't gladly relinquish either.

Rhythmic form and subject-matter are locked in a permanent embrace : that should be an axiom nowadays. So, in metrical verse, it is the nature of the control being exercised that becomes part of the life being spoken about. It is poetry making great use of the conscious intelligence, but its danger is bombast—the controlling music drowning out everything else. Free verse invites a different style of experience, improvisation. *Its* danger lies in being too relaxed, too lacking in controlling energy. For me, at any rate, but I think my generalizations extend somewhat beyond my own practice.

In the first half of the sixties, though, little of the poetry I wrote satisfied me. Much of it was simply lacking in intensity. I was having difficulty in shaping the new 'humane impulse' into anything worth reading; I was having difficulty too, in understanding what *I* could do with free verse.

There was one poem I was working on with which I had a different kind of problem, though it turned out, simply, to be a matter of scale. The poem was about a man who supposes he is the last survivor of a massive global war, and about his surprise on seeing from the hill where he sits a group of refugees approaching on the plain beneath. My trouble with it, I began to realize, was that there was too much exposition for me to cram into a single short poem. Then somewhat later, while making a lengthy recovery from hepatitis, I fell on the notion that perhaps I could extend it into a long poem, or rather a series of linked poems in different forms that would add up to a narrative. This is how 'Misanthropos' came about. Many of the themes and ideas in the poem originated in, or were at least helped along by, the wide-ranging discussions between my friends Don Doody and Tony Tanner, some of them across the bed of my recuperation. I conceived of the work at times as science fiction and at times as pastoral: there is something from William Golding's *The Inheritors* in it and there is also an Elizabethan echo song. The hill to which the last man has retreated shares characteristics with both Ladd's Hill in North Kent and Land's End in San Francisco.

I spent about two years over the whole poem, starting it in San Francisco and finishing it in London, where I spent a year of great happiness from mid-1964 to 1965. I was living on Talbot Road, a few blocks from my friend Tony White, in a large room on the second floor of a handsome Victorian house that has since been torn down. He was translating books from French into English at that time; we would work all morning in our respective rooms and then at midday emerge on our balconies where we would signal to each other (through binoculars) if we wanted to go for a beer and lunch together. London had never seemed more fertile: I think of that twelve months as moving to the tunes of the Beatles, for it started with their movie *A Hard Day's Night* and was punctuated by the rebellious joy of their singles. They stood for a great optimism, barriers seemed to be coming down all over, it was as if World War II had finally drawn to its close, there was an openness and high-spiritedness and relaxation of mood I did not remember from the London of earlier years. The last week I was there, an old woman across the street had what I took to be her grandson from the country staying with her. In the long summer evenings the boy would sit at a window gazing at what went on below him on Talbot Road. He sticks in my mind as an emblem of the potential and excitement and sense of wonder that I found all about me in the London of that year.

It was during this time I made a recording for the British Council which later got issued as part of a record, *The Poet Speaks*, shared with Ted Hughes, Sylvia Plath, and Peter Porter (though we were all four taped on separate occasions). I have made other records at different times: all are terrible, either because I was not reading at my best or because of the conditions of recording. *The Poet Speaks* is the only one that I like.

And I saw a lot of my brother and his family, who were living in Teddington. Looking through some of Ander's photographs I found interesting possibilities in a collaboration. I had always wanted to work with pictures, and he was taking just the kind that made a good starting point for my imagination. That was the beginning of the book called *Positives* (the title being Tony White's suggestion, as was much else in it). I was never very sure whether what I was writing opposite the photographs were poems or captions—they were somewhere between the two, I suspect—but that didn't matter, because what I was looking for was a form of fragmentary inclusiveness that could embody the detail and history of that good year. At the same time I was consciously borrowing what I could from William Carlos Williams, trying as it were to anglicize him, to help make his openness of form and feeling available to English writers. I enjoyed working on the book, the only collaboration I have yet tried, and it contains a London I found hard to recognize only eight years after.

So when I returned to San Francisco it was with half thoughts of ultimately moving back to London. But San Francisco in mid-1965 was only a little behind London in the optimism department and was prepared to go much further. It was the time, after all, not only of the Beatles but of LSD as well. Raying out from the private there was a public excitement at the new territories that were being opened up in the mind. Golden Gate Park, the scene of so many mass trips and rock concerts, seemed like

> The first field of a glistening continent
> Each found by trusting Eden in the human.

We tripped also at home, on rooftops, at beaches and ranches, some went to the opera loaded on acid, others tried it as passengers on gliders, every experience was illuminated by the drug. (The best account of these years in San Francisco is to be found in issue no. 207 of the *Rolling Stone*, a brilliant history put together ten years later.) These were the fullest years of my life, crowded with discovery both inner and outer, as we moved between ecstasy and understanding. It is no longer fashionable to praise LSD, but I have no doubt at all that it has been of the utmost importance to me, both as a man and as a poet. I learned from it, for example, a lot of information about myself that I had somehow blocked from my own view. And almost all of the poems that were to be in my next book, *Moly*, written between 1965 and 1970, have in some way however indirect to do with it.

The acid experience was essentially non-verbal. Yet it was clearly important, and I have always believed that it should be possible to write poetry about any subject that was of importance to you. Eventually a friend, Belle Randall, and I decided that it was time to stop generalizing the origin of the acid poem. (Her book that resulted from this decision was *101 Different Ways of Playing Solitaire*, not published until 1973.) By 1968 taking the drug was no longer an unusual experience, probably hundreds of thousands had had at least one experience with it, and many more knew about it without having taken it, so to write about its effects was not any more to be obscure or to make pretentious claims to experience closed to most readers.

Metre seemed to be the proper form for the LSD-related poems, though at first I didn't understand why. Later I rationalized about it thus. The acid trip is unstructured, it opens you up to countless possibilities, you hanker after the infinite. The only way I could give myself any control over the presentation of these experiences, and so could be true to them, was by trying to render the infinite through the finite, the unstructured through the structured. Otherwise there was the danger of the experience's becoming so distended that it would simply unravel like fog before wind in the unpremeditated movement of free verse. Thomas Mann, speaking about how he wrote *Doctor Faustus*, tells of 'filtering' the character of the genius-composer through the more limited but thus more precise consciousness of the bourgeois narrator. I was perhaps doing something like Mann.

I had meanwhile left Berkeley, in 1966, a year after I had been given tenure. After that I taught intermittently at other institutions but now in the late 1970s I am teaching at Berkeley again, though for only one quarter a year and without tenure.

Around 1968 I finally began to learn how to give a poetry reading. Before that I had been petrified with fright at standing in front of an audience reading my own work (strange, since I was not nervous at teaching classes). But in this year I gave a series of readings on the California poetry circuit. Doing so many of them made me lose my nervousness and I was enabled to study the pacing and presentation of a public reading. I realized that I am so far from being an actor and am gifted with so monotonous and limited a voice that I can afford to dramatize my work as much as I want and still will not seem over-dramatic. And I learned that I should treat a poetry reading not as a recital for a bunch of devotees, which my audiences were clearly not, but more as an entertainment—an advertisement for poetry as a whole.

It was toward the end of the sixties that I began to see something of Robert Duncan, though I had first met him quite a few years before. If a certain amount of mutual influence has taken place, it may sound rather as if Fulke Greville and Shelley had been contemporaries capable of learning from each other. Would that they had been.

What Duncan has stressed is the importance of the *act* of writing. It is a reach into the unknown, an adventuring into places you cannot have predicted, where you may find yourself using limbs and organs you didn't know you possessed. Of course, all poets have always known that such adventuring is a normal part of the exercise and procedure of the imagination, but in the last few decades its importance had been minimized in favour of the end result, 'the poem on the page'. Duncan sees the adventure as ongoing, unfinished and unfinishable, and the poem on the page as marking only one stage in it.

Because of a job at Princeton I was able to live in New York for the first half of 1970, something I had always wanted to do for a while. It started unpromisingly enough at the Albert, a hotel for 'transients and residents', most of them under twenty or over sixty. My room was twice broken into during the weeks I was there. But then I was lucky enough to sublease a loft on Prince Street for the rest of my time in New York. It was about 125 feet in length and still rather bare though fitted up with a bathroom and kitchen: it was the best place I have ever lived in. I didn't even mind the large numbers of mice or the smells from the bakery that filled the place in the early hours of the morning. As I had caught Talbot Road at the moment of change, so I caught So Ho just as it stopped being an Italian neighbourhood: the first art gallery appeared round the corner while I lived there. I enjoyed living by myself for six months among the iron architecture, working only two days a week at Princeton, writing a little but reading a lot, and running loose in the West Village every night.

But the mood was changing everywhere. It was the time of numerous bombings—I saw a rather famous town-house go up in smoke—and of the invasion of Cambodia. The feeling of the country was changing, and one didn't know into what. I went back to England for a few months of the summer, and when I returned to San Francisco I felt something strange there too: there was a certain strain in attempting to preserve the euphoria of the sixties, one's anxieties seemed obstructive. I had a couple of rather bad trips on LSD that taught me no end of unpalatable facts about myself, to my great edification.

But my life insists on continuities—between America and England, between free verse and metre, between vision and everyday consciousness. So, in the sixties, at the height of my belief in the possibilities of change, I knew that we all continue to carry the same baggage: in my world, Christian does not shed his burden, only his attitude to it alters. And now that the great sweep of the acid years is over, I cannot unlearn the things that I learned during them, I cannot deny the vision of what the world might be like. Everything that we glimpsed—the trust, the brotherhood, the repossession of innocence, the nakedness of spirit—is still a possibility and will continue to be so.

In the early seventies I went a few times with friends to the area in Sonoma County, north of San Francisco, known as the Geysers. Some hundred or more people camped there at weekends, fewer stayed through the week. We camped anywhere, on the flanks of the hills, which were warm even at night, or in the woodland, or beside the cool and the warm streams. Everyone walked around naked, swimming in the cool stream by day and at night staying in the hot baths until early in the morning. Heterosexual and homosexual orgies sometimes overlapped: there was an attitude of benevolence and understanding on all sides that could be extended, I thought, into the rest of the world. When I remember that small, changing society of holidays and weekends, I picture a great communal embrace. For what is the point of a holiday if we cannot carry it back into working days? There is no good reason why that hedonistic and communal love of the Geysers could not be extended to the working life of the towns. Unless it is that human beings contain in their emotions some homeostatic device by which they must defeat themselves just as they are learning their freedom.

I wrote a group of poems about this place. Around the same time I was working on another, very loose group of short poems, to do with nightmare, which I called 'Jack Straw's Castle'. The poems were fragmentary, barely connected, and grotesque. Then what had happened with 'Misanthropos' ten years before happened again—'Jack Straw' developed into a narrative. The result was the obverse of the Geyser poems, in that, while in them I had been writing largely about escapes from the confinement of the individual consciousness, I was here dealing with just that confinement and with the terrors of self-destructiveness you may face when you are aware of being trapped in your own skull.

The myth behind the narrative had emerged in the following way. After living for ten years on Filbert Street, I had made the down-payment for a house on Cole Street on the other side of San Francisco, in a district which at that time had become very unfashionable. There were now three of us, but the process of moving our things and remodelling some of the house took us about a month in all. It thereupon became for me the theme of several months of anxiety-dreams. In them I was constantly finding that something had gone wrong with the moving: I had moved into the wrong house, for example, or it was an unrecognizable house, or I was sharing it with strangers (once Nixon turned up in my room), or—and this was the most common dream of all—I had moved into the right house but in it I found *new rooms* that I had known nothing about. It is a strange fact that almost everything that figures importantly in my life, an event, an idea, even a series of dreams, finds its way sooner or later into poetry.

Writing poetry has in fact become a certain stage in my coping with the world, or in the way I try to understand what happens to me and inside me. Perhaps I could say that my poetry is an attempt to *grasp*, with grasp meaning both to *take hold of* in a first bid at possession, and also to *understand*. I certainly do not pretend that I ever do completely possess or understand, I can only say that I attempt to. Often it will be a long time before I can write of something. It took me years before I could begin writing about my father (and maybe I can one day write about my mother—if Duncan has not already written the ultimate mother-poem with his 'My Mother Would be a Falconress'). But sometimes I can write about something more quickly. When Pretty Jim stole from his friends, and when I heard about the odd definition of trust he had made a few days before, 'an intimate conspiracy', I puzzled until out of my puzzlement I wrote 'The Idea of Trust'. I like this poem because in it I ended up with more sympathy for him than I started with, and consequently writing it minutely altered me, advanced my understanding in one small area. So, for all my many dry periods, I must count my writing as an essential part of the way in which I deal with my life.

I am however a rather derivative poet. I learn what I can from whom I can, mostly consciously. I borrow heavily from my reading because I take my reading seriously: it is part of my total experience and I base most of my poetry on my experience. I do not apologize for being derivative because I think a lot of other poets work in this way. I wonder if the real difference between the 'plagiarist' and the Ben Jonson who 'rearranges' Philostratus into 'Drink to me only with thine eyes' is more between degrees of talent than between degrees of borrowing. Specifically, I have found usable modes in the work of other poets, and I have tried to invent some myself. Moreover, it has not been of primary interest to develop a unique poetic personality, and I rejoice in Eliot's lovely remark that art is the escape from personality. This lack in me has troubled some readers.

What more do I have to say about my life? I still live in San Francisco, and expect to go on living there. I visit England every three or four years, to see what has been happening to my friends and relatives. My income averages about half of that of a local bus driver or street sweeper, but it is of my own choosing, since I prefer leisure to working at a full-time job. I do not either like or dislike myself inordinately. I have just had *Jack Straw's Castle and Other Poems* published. I cannot guess what my next book will be like.

Postscript

I have written the foregoing because the authors of this biblio-graphy[1] asked me to and they are nice men whom I would like to please. Another reason is that if I don't do it, someone else will, sooner or later, and he is likely to get it wrong. And another is that true history, like true gossip, is always of some interest. All this even though I have been reticent in the past, perhaps rather self-importantly exaggerating the desirability of my privacy. But there was another reason, a good one, for reticence, and I should like to conclude by explaining it.

The danger of biography, and equally of autobiography, is that it can muddy poetry by confusing it with its sources. James's word for the source of a work, its 'germ', is wonderfully suggestive be-cause the source bears the same relation to the finished work as the seed does to the tree—nothing is the same, all has developed, the historical truth of the germ is superseded by the derived but completely different artistic truth of the fiction.

Isherwood recently published a volume of autobiography, *Christopher and His Kind*. It is a book that I wouldn't wish un-written for anything. But it is sure to confuse his novels and stories for the many people who prefer speculation to reading what is in front of them. They can say that Sally Bowles, for example, isn't *really* doing whatever she is clearly doing in the story, because in his autobiography Isherwood himself may have told us something additional or even contrary about Jean Ross, the original of Sally.

Here's an example of the kind of misunderstanding I'm talking about: what does it do if I say of a poem called 'From an Asian Tent' that in it I am finally able to write about my father? My admission confuses matters, I think, being misleading both about the poem and about my relationship with my father. I would like the poem read as being about what it proclaims as its subject: Alexander the Great remembering Philip of Macedon. What is autobiographical about the poem, what I am drawing upon, is a secret source of feeling that might really be half-imagined, some Oedipal jealousy for my father combined with a barely remembered but equally strong incestuous desire for him. And I am drawing

---

[1] This essay was written as a biographical introduction to *Thom Gunn: A Bibliography, 1940–1978*, compiled by Jack W. C. Hagstrom and George Bixby, London (Bertram Rota), 1979. [Ed.]

upon the autobiographical without scruple, freed by the myth from any attempt to be fair or honest about my father. The poem's truth is in its faithfulness to a possibly imagined feeling, not to my history.

Another example. In my early twenties I wrote a poem called 'Carnal Knowledge', addressed to a girl, with a refrain making variations on the phrase 'I know you know'. Now anyone aware that I am homosexual is likely to misread the whole poem, inferring that the thing 'known' is that the speaker would prefer to be in bed with a man. But that would be a serious misreading, or at least a serious misplacement of emphasis. The poem, actually addressed to a fusion of two completely different girls, is not saying anything as clear-cut as that. A reader knowing nothing about the author has a much better chance of understanding it.

Theodore Dreiser, 1943